[handwritten inscription] Linda Welcome to Matza 101 Jenny Kdoshim

W9-AMB-277

Matza 101

An Innovative COOKBOOK Containing "101" Creative Recipes Simply Made With MATZA!

Jenny Kdoshim and Debbie Bevans

Jenny Kdoshim and Debbie Bevans are pleased to present the Third edition of

MATZA 101

North American Distribution by Alef Judaica, Inc.
Culver City, California 90232

(310) 202-0024

All rights reserved. No part of this publication may be translated, reproduced, stored in a retrieval system or transmitted, in any form or by any means, electronic, mechanical, photocopying, recording or otherwise, without express written permission from the publishers.

ISBN: 0 - 9646564 - 2- 6

Library of Congress Card Catalog:

Copyright © 1997 by Jenny Kdoshim and Debbie Bevans

All rights reserved, including the right to reproduce in whole or in part

To our devoted families, for their encouragement, patience, and support throughout the workings and writings of Matza 101. We would like to thank our husbands Bruyn and Prosper for their honesty and for enduring two years of meals made with simply matza. It was their encouragement that helped bring this unique cookbook into a reality. To our food critics since they began teething, our children, Leah, Jessica, Shana, and Leiat

To the home cooks that brought a need for new ideas during the Passover holidays

On a personal note, we would like to thank G-D, for planting an original, untouched idea within us in order to become an instrument in your kitchen and to bring our families one step closer...

FORWARD...

With the coming of the Passover holidays, we are pleased to offer a special cookbook whose recipes are based on the unleavened bread, MATZA, which is eaten the eight days of Passover instead of ordinary bread. Although the laws of Passover are the same for all Jews, there are many customs which vary from community to community and even from one family to another. Sephardic Jews permit the use of rice and beans. Ashkenazic Jews do not. Many people permit the use of matza in cooked foods. Some permit this only on the last day of Passover. When in doubt about any laws or customs of Passover, one should ask an Orthodox Rabbi.

Of course all ingredients must bear a reliable seal of approval that they are kosher for Passover. Wishing all our readers a kosher and happy Passover.

Jenny Y. Kdoshim

Deborah R. Bevans

Introduction...

We suppose the most common asked question is "Why a cookbook with just Matza?" The answer is quite simple and you could probably identify with us.

We both enjoy cooking and don't have any problems coming up with meals on a daily basis. But, when Passover rolls around, we are posed with wanting to try various different dishes. Psychologically we limit our cooking power and abilities because we cannot use leavened bread. We open the refrigerator and stare with a GRAND question mark!

Well, time has come to unleash the power of cooking not only for Passover, but for the entire year. You will find that working with Matza is easier and you will refer to your new cookbook for recipes throughout the year.

Now, we were faced with attempting a new and acceptable venture with success. Needless to say, as we were writing we kept it quiet until we were certain that we were on the right track. At the tail end we introduced our idea to friends and they were thrilled; which by normal means would have been adequate incentive for us, but it was not good enough. When we discussed this new concept with various women at WOMEN GROUPS and saw that the response was "HURRY AND FINISH", then we knew we were on a trail of No Return...

This all began when we created Matza Cheese Lasagna made with plain sheets of matza. We then thought how wonderful it would be to have a cookbook that had various recipes with "Just Matza". We discovered there was no such book, as of this writing, anywhere in the world! And this now was our incentive to begin.

Next question, how many recipes would we be able to pull together, and will this be possible being that Passover has limits on the food that we are allowed to eat. Our original thought was to use simple plain sheets of matza... But, we then discovered that we could manipulate the matza cracker by using paper towels and water. And well, more incentive to continue. It now became apparent that this book would become possible and the ideas now became endless... hence, MATZA 101 was created. Meet the authors, and read how we pulled this project off!

***We are pleased to be in your home and celebrate true freedom.
May we all be together, "Next Year in Jerusalem"***

Meet The Authors

Jenny Kdoshim, (pictured on the right) Born in Israel, April 21, 1961. Immigrated to the U.S. at age 8. Married 16 years, 1 daughter. Full time computer/software technician. Enjoys painting, chess, music, outdoor activities, and naturally computers! Cooking exotic dishes has been a form of expression and relaxation for Jenny.

Debbie Bevans, (pictured on the left) Born in Van Nuys, California, May 7, 1956. Grew up in California. Married 19 years, 3 daughters. Full time Homemaker. Enjoys exercise, gardening, music, and naturally cooking! Baking is Debbie's specialty and form of creative expression.

Ever wonder what to do with Matza? Cooking is second nature for these two women living next door to each other.   They were friends before they became neighbors -- Risky Business! Their culinary talent derives from mothers of earlier generations that did not use any form of measurement.   Science in the kitchen equated to "a little of this, or a little of that!" Even more cause of degree, is their greatest food critics since they began teething, their children. These two women have developed a process in which you can manipulate this wonderful flat matza cracker, better known as the bread of affliction, and created a smorgasbord of recipes from Baklava and Cannolies to Knishes and Giflte Fish Enchiladas.

The two worked on the creation of Matza 101 late hours of the night and had to function normally the following day. Unfortunately there are only 24 hours in a day, but fortunately there was a 24 hour supermarket around the corner and plenty of computers to work with. After dinner, homework with the girls, and family time, the creation of Matza 101 began. Signals were used in the middle of the night at about 12:30 AM from either window. One would use the phone to call the other and let the phone ring once and hang up. That signal meant for the other to go to the window and if the light was turned on and off in the kitchen or the office, then that meant the coast was clear. They would then meet out front, go to the market, and pick up the various ingredients for a new recipe. The cooking went on well into the morning hours. Each knew their role in this melange of frenzy. The cooking and baking was created together as well as the wonderful clean up. The last step was to download the information into the computer. The following day was testing on their families, matza recipes. This went on for THREE years.   No one seemed to mind, in fact they got used to matza rather quickly.   It now became apparent to these two women that this cookbook would become possible and the ideas became endless... hence, Matza 101 was created. And by the way, they are still neighbors, and now are business partners!

Publishing a cookbook was not an ordinary task for these two women, but with determination they persevered and researched the market needs and found no other cookbook that had recipes containing only matza -- now that was unique! Four years in the making and research, Jenny and Debbie bring you MATZA 101...

Table Of Contents

Helpful Hints   26

Preparation Process   33

Fish/Kugels/Casseroles/Dairy

Matza Cheese Lasagna	42
Matza Eggplant Lasagna	43
Matza Gefilte Fish Enchiladas	44
Matza `N` Cheese Casserole	45
Matza Potato Knishes	46
Matza Veggie Calzones	47
Matza Asparagus Crispers	48
Matza Egg Folds	49
Matza Stuffers, Italian Style	50
Matza Lasagna Spinach Rolls	51
Matza Broccoli Cheese Casserole	52
Matza Cannelloni	53
Matza Chili Pepper Rellenos	54
Matza Vegetable Cheese Quesadilla	55
Matza Asparagus Swiss Quiche	56
Matza Broccoli Quiche	57
Matza Spinach Quiche	58
Matza Banana Blintzes	59
Matza Caramel Pears Al-Dente	60
Matza Cheese Blintzes	61

Matza Fruit Kugel   62

Matza Sweet Kugel   63

Matza Fruit Pancakes   64

Matza Savory Pancakes   65

Matza Brei   66

Matza Brei Savory Style   67

Matza Salmon Carousels   68

Matza Salmon Pockets   69

Matza Tuna Casserole   70

Matza Tuna Bakes   71

Matza Tuna Tostadas   72

Matza Asparagus Rolls   73

Matza Cinnamon Toast Popover   74

Matza Breakfast Spirals   75

Matza Borekas   76

Matza `N` Cheese Star Appetizers   77

Matza Cream Cheese `N` Onion   78

Matza Cream Cheese Surprises   79

Matza Garlic Parmesan "Krispers   80

Matza Garlic Teasers   81

Matza Jalapeno Pockets   82

Matza Mozzarella Melts   83

Matza Pizza Pizza Squares   84

Matza Pizzzz-A Pockets   85

Matza Salsa Cream Cheese Mousse   86

Matza Spring Rolls   87

Matza Taco Shells   88

Matza Tortilla Chips   89

Meat And Poultry

Matza Beef `N` Potato Turnovers   92

Matza beef pot pies   93

Matza Meat Cigars   94

Matza Mini Franks   95

Matza Meat Knishes   96

Matza Chili Pepper Chicken   97

Matza Chicken Bastilla Flags   98

Matza Chicken Bastilla   99

Matza Chicken Pot Pies   100

Matza Tex-Mex Chicken   101

Matza Turkey Rolls   102

Desserts

Matza Almond Cookies   104

Matza Almond Squares   105

Matza Apple Strudel   106

Matza Apple/Cinnamon Broilers   107

Matza Baklava   108

Matza Banana Nut Broilers   109

Matza Brown Sugar Cookies   110

Matza Crystallized Nuts   111

Matza Cannolies   112

Matza Chocolate Cherry Bars   113

Matza Chocolate Chip Cookies   114

Matza Chocolate Clusters   115

Matza Chocolate Glazed Cookies   116

Matza Cherry Jubilee Cookies   117

Matza Date Mousse Puffs   118

Matza Florentines   119

Matza Fondue Strips   120

Matza Haroseth Cookie Rolls   121

Matza Honey Chewies   122

Matza Honey Nut Strudel   123

Matza 'Jammer' Cookies   124

Matza Mock Maple `N` Nut Crunch   125

Matza Napoleon   126

Matza Newtons   127

Matza Pecan Brown Sugar Crunchies   128

Matza Pineapple Strudel   129

Matza Sesame Teasers   130

Matza Old Fashioned Taiglach   131

Matza Vanilla Crisps   132

Matza Ice Cream Sandwiches   133

Matza Walnut Bon Bons   134

Matza N.Y. Cheese Cake   135

Matza Apple Tart   137

Matza Chocolate Berry Tart   138

Matza Fresh Fruit Tart   139

Matza Maple Pecan Tart   140

Matza Peach Raspberry Tart   141

Matza Strawberry Tarts   142

Matza Brownie Walnut Pie   143

Matza Lemon Meringue Pie   144

Matza Pear/Apple Crumb Pie   145

Matza Walnut Wheels   146

Diagrams   *147*

Index   *153*

Photographs By: John S. Reid

Everything Else We Thank Various Family Members, Including Scott And Us, The Partners!

Measurement Table

OVEN TEMPERATURES: Throughout Matza 101 temperatures are given in degrees Fahrenheit. The following chart gives the conversions from degrees Fahrenheit to degrees Centigrade:

°F	°C	
225	110	Very cool or very slow
250	130	
275	140	Cool or slow
300	150	
325	170	Very moderate
350	180	Moderate
375	190	Moderately hot
400	200	
425	220	Hot
450	230	Very hot
475	240	

METRIC MEASURES: The following table shows conversion to metric measures for working equivalent:

American	Metric
1 ounce	28 Grams
1 pound	450 Grams
1 teaspoon	5 milliliters
1 tablespoon	15 milliliters
1 cup	210 grams
1 inch	2.5 centimeters

Weights and Measure

3 teaspoons = 1 tablespoon * 4 tablespoons = 1/4 cup * 5 1/3 tablespoons = 1/3 cup
8 tablespoons = 1/2 cup * 10 2/3 tablespoons = 2/3 cup * 12 tablespoons = 3/4 cup
16 tablespoons = 1 cup

Matza Baklava

Baklava originates from Turkey. Turkey is a Middle Eastern nation that lies both in Europe and in Asia. Turkey borders Bulgaria on the northwest; Greece on the west; Georgia, Armenia, Azerbaijan, and Iran on the east; and Iraq and Syria on the south. The Black Sea lies to the north, the Aegean Sea to the west, and the Mediterranean Sea to the north.

The location explains the popularity of Baklava within its surrounding country. Many of these countries have adopted this fantastic pastry and have made minor alterations. You will find many Middle Eastern recipes throughout Matza 101.

Baklava is a popular dessert made of thin layers of pastry, honey, and chopped nuts. Commonly used dough is phyllo. Of course we had to include this popular pastry in Matza 101. We have found that after you prepare the matza, you can roll it thin and prepare the Baklava as you would using phyllo dough. It is a very simple process and is quite appealing. Anyone that has made Baklava will appreciate the simplicity.

Baklava is such a rich pastry that we suggest to simply serve it with a good cup of mint tea...

ENJOY!

Matza Taco Shells...

Taco Shells originate from Mexico. Mexico is the northernmost country of Latin America. It lies just south of the United States.

Taco shells are made with corn meal. The main corn meal food in Mexico is the tortilla, a thin flat bread shaped by hand or machine. Tortilla is the main bread of Mexicans. Tortillas can also be made with wheat flour. The taco is a folded tortilla and is filled with either meat, chicken or cheese.

You will find a few Mexican recipes throughout Matza 101. Some of these include: Matza Tortilla Chips, Tostadas, Chili Pepper Rellenos, and of coarse Matza Tacos. We chose some of these Mexican foods because the spices mixed into the matza create a wonderful flavor.

We found that serving Matza tacos stuffed with tuna serves well for a light meal. You can, of course, stuff these wonderful folds with basically anything savory. We suggest that you serve Matza tacos with a green salad and our taco tortilla chips.

Side garnish would include tomatoes, avocado, sour cream, salsa, green peppers, olives...

ENJOY!

Matza Cheese Blintzes...

Blintzes originated from the Ukraine. Ukraine is the second largest country in area in Europe. Ukraine lies in southeastern Europe and borders the Black Sea.

Blintzes are a thin rolled pancake filled with some soft foods such as cheese, jam, or fruit. You can easily compare a Blintz to the French Crepe.

Blintzes have become a traditional recipe throughout many households as a Sunday brunch. Blintzes have become a main dairy food during the holiday, Shavuot.

We have suggested that you fill blintzes with cheese, but there are many variations such as fresh fruit - blue berries and apples. If you are going to stuff blintzes with cheese, then simply serve with fresh fruit on the side. You can also simplify this recipe by filling with just cottage cheese and sugar - omit the egg - and see how simple and delicious! Try serving blintzes for breakfast, and receive a gourmet response...

ENJOY!

Matza Chicken Bastilla Flags...

Chicken Bastilla originates from Morocco. Morocco is a country in the northwestern corner of Africa. It is bordered by the Mediterranean Sea on the north and the Atlantic Ocean on the west.

Bastilla is made with phyllo dough and is formed into a pie pan.   It is then filled with chicken, almonds, sugar, and eggs. This may sound like a crazy combination, but it truly is a wonderful melange of ingredients. Now Chicken Bastilla flags are pretty much the same type of filling, only simpler to prepare. Matza Bastilla and Bastilla flags are wonderfully different. We suggest that you serve Bastilla flags as either an appetizer or a main dish with salad...

Also featured in our photo are Chicken Pot Pies - and well, that is as American as we get. Pot pies can be stuffed with any leftover meat and also serve well with a salad...

ENJOY!

Fish... Kugels... Casseroles... And Dairy...

Pictured Top Center Is Our Cheese Lasagna - We guarantee that you will make lasagna with matza from now on. This is one of the easiest recipes to make. You will use sheets of matza directly from the box and begin layering. The matza will absorb the sauce and become a noodle type texture. Serve with salad containing lettuce greens, walnuts, and apples topped with a light Italian dressing (use lemon).

Pictured Center Left Is Our Cream Cheese And Onion Bakes - These are great for a simple after school snack. Serve with steamed vegetables.

Pictured Center Right Is Our Asparagus Swiss Quiche - There are many variations of quiches. We made a few simple ones for you to try. Quiches serve well with a Greek Salad containing lettuce greens, red onions, black olives, tomatoes, feta cheese topped with a light Italian dressing. And why not add fresh fruit...

Pictured Bottom Center are Borekas - Most popular and sold in most corner vendors in Israel and loved by all ages, Borekas are usually made with a puff pastry dough. There are various types of fillings for borekas that range from cheeses to meats, we suggest the feta cheese filling. Try sautéing onions and mushrooms and stuff with mashed potatoes. Serve as an appetizer with olives, and pickles or as a meal with a salad.

Enjoy...

Meat And Poultry...

Pictured top Center Are Our Meat Cigars - You will find this delightful appetizer in most Sephardic homes during the holidays. Cigars are shaped as such and are filled with spicy meat. The dough for the cigars is similar to phyllo dough. Try this simple version with prepared matza!

Pictured Center Left Is Our Chicken Bastilla - A combination of chicken, scrambled eggs, walnuts, almonds and powdered sugar. Sounds strange? This is definitely a meal in one worth trying.

Pictured Center right Are Tortilla Chips - Tortilla chips are simple to make with matza. You can flavor with any of your favorite toppings including spicy ingredients. You'll find that the recipe calls for layering the chips on a single cookie sheet, but you can place the flavored chips together in a big baking pan and cook at a low degree oven (300) for a couple of hours, turning every 20 minutes. This is a way to take advantage of an entire box of matza just for tortilla chips. Store the chips in a plastic bag. The chips will keep in an air tight baggy for up to two months!

Pictured Center Bottom Is Our Chili Pepper Chicken - What a way to use leftovers! We used chicken, flavored it, rolled it into a matza, topped it with a sauce and bake. This you can essentially do with any leftovers...

Enjoy...

Desserts...

Top center are our various matza cookies- Most of the cookies can be made with the matza scraps. You can be as fancy as you'd like. Simply shape your sweet scraps to the desired shapes, bake on a flat cookie sheet in a 375 degree oven, let cool: dip into chocolate and roll in some toasted assorted nuts or coconut!

Pictured middle center are our napoleons - Usually napoleons are made with a puff pastry. You can make the rectangular shapes by starting from scratch or you may have some scraps saved from other sweet recipes. Making napoleons with matza is not an issue anymore.

Pictured center left are our strawberry tarts - The easiest way to make smaller bite size tarts is to simply use one prepared matza sheet, flavor with the sweet mixture (sugar, orange juice, vanilla), and cut up small circles, about 2" diameter. Place the circled matza into a muffin pan, the one made for small muffins (12 to 1 pan) and bake in a preheated oven for 20 minutes. Simply remove while they are hot, let cool and stuff with most anything. We suggest a sweet cream cheese filling topped with a strawberry or fresh fruit. Try placing melted chocolate on the bottom topped with a raspberry. Or bake brownie mix into the tart... we can go on and we're sure you will...

Pictured center right are our Cannolies - Well worth purchasing the cannoli tubes. For a different variation, try using the savory seasonings for the cannoli and stuff with sautéed onions and mushrooms...

Pictured center bottom is our fresh fruit tart - Make the tart shell and basically use your favorite tart recipe for this one!!!

Enjoy...

Helpful Hints

Matza 101 is a course involving 101 various recipes using simply matza. We don't profess to be Grammar majors, but we feel that we are very descriptive with our recipes. After all this is a cookbook, and writing space is limited. It's a good thing that only the writing is limited and not the recipes. THE FOLLOWING ARE SOME VERY HELPFUL HINTS FOR YOUR COURSE AND ARE REQUIRED TO BE READ FOR A SUCCESSFUL RESULT IN PREPARING THE MATZA

Matza

When purchasing your Matza, we suggest that you buy the thicker type of matza that contain No Oils. If you purchase the most popular American Brand Name of matza and paper towels, you should have no problems with the process. The thicker the matza, the better it will absorb and become easy to work with. You will find some boxes that will contain cracked matza, in which case, you could use that box for the recipes that call for dry cracked matza. We don't suggest that you process cracked matza because you will find yourself becoming aggravated. Be sure the matza you use is fresh -- OLD MATZA WILL BREAK OFF.

After matza has been prepared, many of our recipes require cutting up and trimming. So, now you ask, "What do I do with the scraps?". We have plenty of recipes that deal with matza scraps, especially casseroles. You will not waste one bit of matza. Check out our KUGEL recipes or use with your favorite kugel recipe in place of noodles. Simply reserve the scraps in a plastic baggy and store in the refrigerator for later use.

When you do come across a recipe that requires you to use matza scraps, be sure to compact the scraps when measuring.

Read First

Before attempting any of the recipes, read through first. Pay special attention to line ingredients. Our aim was to fit one recipe per page. In order to do this, we had to squeeze a couple of items onto one line to avoid pages from overlapping. Some of these recipes require advance time for preparation and possibly special cooking tools.

If the ends of the matza are burnt, then be sure to trim all sides, even if the recipe does not call for it. The purpose for this is to avoid bitter tasting dishes.

Margarine

Butter is the fat of choice for a rich flavor, but who are we kidding? We use margarine throughout Matza 101, but it can be interchangeably used. You can also use margarine substitutes such as spreads because they contain less fat and more water. If you are going to use a spread be sure that is contains no less than 60 percent vegetable oil or it will affect the texture and quality of the baked recipes.

Definitely use Non-stick cooking spray to avoid the mess of greasing pans. Be sure to use the cooking spray on cold baking pans and skillets.

Softened margarine is one of the KEY ingredients throughout MATZA 101. It is very important that prior to making any of the recipes that you bring the margarine to room temperature. DO NOT melt the margarine unless specifically asked. We suggest melting the margarine with the other ingredients to top the sweet and savory shell - but first try it the conventional method before getting into melting it all at once. We don't fry or use oil with matza (except a couple of the classic recipes). It was discovered that matza absorbs oil quickly and does not do so well when frying.   We use the concept of spreading softened margarine on the prepared matza, then we bake the coated matza. This acts well in providing us with the fried effect. Besides, this is less of a mess and tastes just the same, if not better. Softened margarine also helps to seal the matza together as required for many of the recipes. NOTE: for the few recipes that do require frying, be sure that the skillet is hot before adding any mixture.

Margarine, Continued...

Preparing the SWEET Recipes, we have found that generously coating the matza cracker with the softened margarine or butter, followed by generously sprinkling with sugar, makes up a delicious full flavored matza. The softened margarine helps to not only brown both our savory and sweet dishes, but it also makes the matza crispy.

Using margarine to coat the matza, we use either a butter knife or pastry brush. Be sure to use a WOODEN CUTTING BOARD. We found less sticking occurs this way. If sticking does occur, then gently use a spatula to lift the matza off of the cutting board. If there is to much sticking, then use less amounts of margarine, this could be caused by the brand name of margarine you use.

Recipes that require large amounts of preparation, can be prepared by using one piece of matza at a time. You don't have to cut the required shapes out all at once. It is suggested that once you have the PREPARED matza, that you cut the matza one at a time, stuff, then place onto cookie sheets.

It is not necessary to coat both sides of matza as described in many of the SAVORY recipes. You can coat the baking dish well with margarine, roll the matza as described, place seam side down, then coat the exposed top by brushing with softened margarine. Be sure to use this short-cut method only with SAVORY dishes.

FOR THE ADVANCED - A quick option for flavoring the matza for the sweet recipes is to melt together the sugar, margarine, and vanilla over a low flame then brush the prepared matza with the flavored margarine. Do the same to flavor the matza for the savory recipes; melt together the margarine, salt, pepper, garlic powder, onion powder, etc. together.

Yield And Storage

You will notice that many of the recipes in MATZA 101 yield a few dozen at a time. This is because many of our recipes store well in airtight containers or in the refrigerator. So, if you have the mess out already, you may as well invest the time to make extra because in many cases it is not worth to make small amounts. If you feel it's to much, then cut the recipe in half. The reverse holds true for smaller recipes; if you want to double up, all that much more.

When you prepare the matza, we suggest to prepare a couple of boxes at a time. You can then store the prepared matza in a plastic bag or wrap it up in plastic and store in the refrigerator for up to four days. You can either store the matza with or without the paper towels. In fact, you will find it easier to work with the matza after it has been refrigerated. Don't worry the matza will not dry out if it is sealed properly.

Freezing is an easy way to preserve your recipes. Freezing the casseroles and Kugels before baking is okay. Freezing many of the cooked savory recipes should be no problem. We don't suggest to freeze the prepared matza. You can freeze using a variety of freezer containers and freezer bags. Freezing time for cooked matza recipes should be no more than 6 weeks. Be sure the food has thoroughly cooled before freezing.

The various baked SHELLS such as the Cannolies, tarts, taco shells, and cookies can all be stored in an airtight bag or container and NOT to be frozen. We found that these items including the taco chips store well for about 2 months in airtight containers.

Tools

We suggest that you use Non-Stick everything! It is easier to clean up and Matza reacts better on these surfaces. Many of the recipes require that you use margarine on your baking tools, this is because the margarine adds to the browning effect. If you don't use non-stick, then place foil over cookie sheets, and spread margarine at all times. The majority of the recipes require that you margarine bottoms of pans regardless of Non-stick label. Try to use large skillets. Unless specified in the recipe, be sure not to over crowd rolled matza in skillets or it will become difficult to turn matza over.

It is suggested that you have a sharp knife, scissors, ravioli cutter or pinking shears for cutting. If you don't have pinking shears, we strongly advise that you make the purchase for appearance sake of many of our dishes; it truly adds a defined finish.

A Food Processor is used throughout MATZA 101 for chopping, crushing, pureeing and even mixing. When a recipe calls for toasted, crushed almonds - be sure to toast the almonds first, then run through a food processor. Use a GARLIC PRESS whenever a recipe calls for pressed garlic.

Baking pans, Casserole pans, and Baking racks are a must. Many of our recipes require the rolling, stuffing and placing. You will find it easy to place the matza into casserole dishes that look good for serving hot out of the oven. Baking racks are used in many of the SWEET recipes for cooling the trimmed matza. Be sure that racks are coated with either butter or margarine to avoid sticking. It's important that ALL cookies be completely cooled before removing from cookie sheets.

Wooden utensils are used versus metal ones. Not only do you want to avoid scratching your pans, but many of the ingredients react better with wooden utensils. To repeat, use a wooden cutting board, or a cold marble pastry board for spreading the softened margarine onto matza.

Tools, Continued...

If you plan, and we suggest that you do, on making Cannolies, then you will need to purchase Cannoli tubes. The tubes are also used for making the Taco Shells. Getting back to using whatever you have in the kitchen -- you can also use a kitchen staple, the great aluminum foil. Simply bunch up some foil and shape it into a cylinder now coat with margarine or non-stick cooking spray, then roll the matza - and this will suffice.

A Candy Thermometer would be beneficial, but not necessary. This is for those of you that want to get into candy making. We do guide you within the individual recipes on how to measure temperature level if you do not have a candy thermometer.

Paper Towels are essential. There is no way around this because the majority of our recipes require that you have PREPARED matza, and part of the preparation of matza is the use of paper towels. Be sure to use thick paper towels. Use only white paper towels with no designs so that you can avoid any possible dyes that may leak onto the matza.

Rolling And Cutting

If you are using a knife to cut the prepared matza, then it is essential that the knife be sharp. Keep your knives in good condition by sharpening them before each use. Cut the prepared matza in a rolling motion. You can also cut the matza by using sharp scissors. Whatever you use, be sure it's sharp to cut with.

Be sure to follow special notes in the directions for the cutting process. Most recipes call for cutting "By following the Grain". The reason for this usually is for rolling the various ingredients involved in the recipe. You will find it easier to roll the matza by "ROLLING AGAINST THE GRAIN". This prevents cracking. Another tip to avoid cracking, is to not overfill the matza. We found it easy to place the matza VERTICALLY in front of you, then roll away from you by going against the grain...

Be sure to always place rolled matza seam-side-down into casserole pans or baking dishes, unless specifically noted.

Baking

When a recipe calls for thorough browning, be sure to do just that. This will allow the matza to remain crisp when cooled. But, when baking cookies (matza rounds), be sure not to over bake, otherwise the matza will taste bitter.

Baking, Continued

When baking, many of the recipes call for toasted nuts as a topping. In that case, be sure that the nuts are lightly toasted, then top. This is to avoid burning the top layer of nuts while the main recipe continues to cook up. When making the pies or tarts, we found an extra flavor is added when you layer first with matza wedges, then top with toasted nuts prior to filling.

Some of our baked recipes require the use of Instant Puddings. A valuable tip is that when working with Instant Pudding, milk should be added in small increments to prevent pudding from becoming gritty.   Pudding tends to lump up when powder is added in all at once to the milk.

We discuss using the muffin pans when making bite size tarts -- We found this to be the simplest method!!!

Final Note

You will notice that after preparing a few of our recipes, we become very redundant in repeating procedures. This is because following directions and maintaining consistency is crucial. This is not an ordinary cookbook. MATZA 101 is unique and there are limited ways in preparing the matza for presentation. And finally...ENJOY!

Matza Preparation Process

Throughout your cookbook you will find recipes that require you to use "Prepared Matza". Preparing the matza is the KEY to making this cookbook successful. There are various ways to prepare the matza. The first one described is our traditional, SIDE BY SIDE method. If this is your first time, we suggest that you use this method to prepare the matza. Once you become more comfortable with the matza process, prepare the matza using the LAYERING method - also very easy, and for us more practical. Be sure to follow the instructions carefully, read thoroughly before beginning the MATZA PROCESS -- Preparing matza takes about 15 - 25 minutes.

When purchasing your matza, you should purchase the most popular American brand name that contains no oils of any form, which should be the thicker matza. Matza is available throughout the year; therefore, finding matza should not be a problem. Purchasing plain matza will insure no problems with our Matza Process. If the matza is cracked in the box, it will remain cracked during process, but that is okay, we have recipes specifically using cracked or broken pieces of matza, so save those scraps.

When purchasing your paper towels, you should purchase the most popular American brand name, which should be the thicker paper towel; again, this will insure ease with our Matza Process.

We really want to emphasize that you don't have to go out of your way to make gourmet type of recipes. In Matza 101 we use whatever tools we have in the kitchen. For example, when asked to cut a round shape out of a sheet of matza, simply use the top of a pot lid or a cereal bowl.

Almost all of the recipes require that you use softened margarine. We found an easier way to do this is to simply melt all of the ingredients down in a small saucepan, then simply brush the matza with the seasoned margarine. We basically use two types of flavors. One is for our sweet shell, which consists of margarine, vanilla, sugar and orange juice. With our savory shell, we use margarine, salt, pepper, garlic powder, onion powder, parsley flakes... or anything else that you may want to add to give it a better flavor. By the way, you can be more creative when you are using matza during the year. By this we suggest to use wines and various liqueurs to flavor the matza - don't limit yourself, we simply gave you a basis to go with. You'll find yourself becoming more creative with matza after making just a few recipe. We have over a hundred more recipes to add, but we wanted to make this cookbook Kosher for Passover.

For more recipes you can subscribe to our Newsletter "Simply Matza", published 6 times a year. Total cost is $12.00. Send payment to: Matza 101, 11785 Mt. Wilson Ct. Alta Loma, CA 91737 - or call for information (909) 483-3902 or E:mail at matza101@AOL.com.

Side By Side Method...

You will need Matza and paper towels.

*

Cover the counter top with heavy duty paper towels. The paper towels are placed on the counter to allow the matza to slowly absorb the water from the paper towels. The trick is wetting the matza and to be sure that the paper towels are wet enough for the matza to absorb the water - this will prevent any type of cracking.

*

Run your tap water at a cool temperature; run one piece of matza through cool tap water, one at a time, making sure you wet both sides. Then place wet matza, side by side, approximately 1/2" apart onto dry paper towels that you have placed on your counter . Repeat this process for remaining matza. Now, place a WET paper (in fact, saturated wet) towel over each wet matza and allow matza to slowly absorb the water from the paper towels. Check about every 5 to 10 minutes until the matza obtains that Al-Dente, lasagna noodle texture. Usual time is about 20 minutes.

*

When you are able to easily bend the sheets of matza, remove the paper towels and allow the matza to stand for about 10 minutes. Again check the matza every 5 minutes or so until it has that Al-Dente, lasagna noodle texture. The drying time of the matza depends upon how thick your paper towels and matza are. Each brand of paper towel absorbs water at a different rate. So, the absorption time for the matza will vary.

*

After the matza has reached that Al-Dente, lasagna noodle type texture, remove paper towels, and let the matza dry for an additional 5-10 minutes -- you are now ready to use the matza for your favorite recipe!

*

At this point if you want you can store the matza in a plastic bag or plastic wrap and store in the refrigerator for later use. Again, do not store more than 4 days. You can store with or without the paper towels...

This procedure is truly very simple. We want you to be successful, this is why we are noting every step in detail. If you have been to our workshops, then you have seen how simple this procedure truly is. For those of you who need to visually see this, we have provided you with photos on the opposite page.

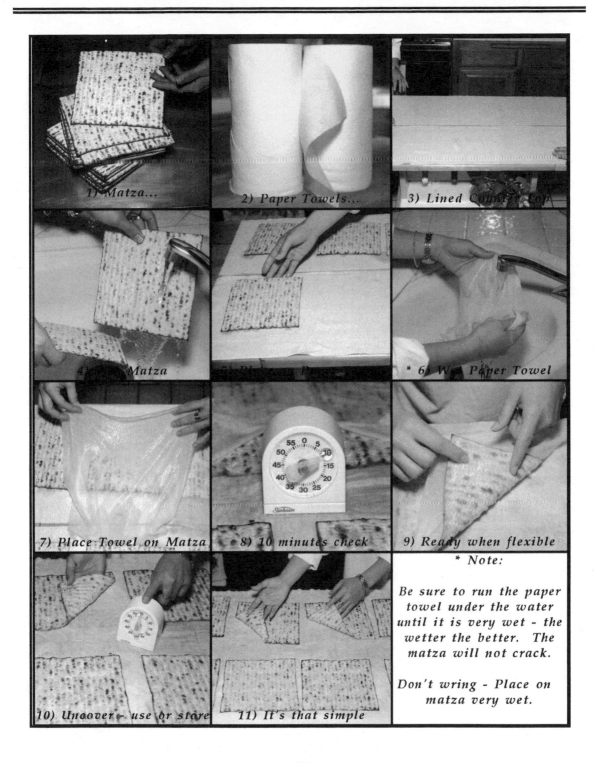

1) Matza...

2) Paper Towels...

3) Lined Counter Top

4) Wet Matza

5) Bedroom Power

* 6) Wet Paper Towel

7) Place Towel on Matza

8) 10 minutes check

9) Ready when flexible

10) Uncover - use or store

11) It's that simple

* Note:

Be sure to run the paper towel under the water until it is very wet - the wetter the better. The matza will not crack.

Don't wring - Place on matza very wet.

Layering Method...

You will need paper towels and matza. With the layering method, you can use one box of matza per batch.

*

Wet both sides of paper towel. Again, be sure to thoroughly wet the paper towels.

*

Place the wet paper towel onto the counter. This method requires that you wet the towel first, versus the dry paper towel discussed with the side by side method. It just works out better this way and eliminates cracking of the first matza.

*

Run your tap water at a cool temperature; run one piece of matza through cool tap water, wetting both sides and place it on top of the wet paper towel. Continue this layering process until you run out of matza. OPTIONAL: After layering all the matza, flip the batch and let stand.

*

Check about every 5 minutes until the matza obtains that Al-Dente, lasagna noodle texture. Usual time is about 15 minutes. You can uncover and let the matza dry for about 10 minutes.

*

You are ready to use the matza for your favorite recipe when you are able to easily bend the sheets of matza as pictured.

*

You can also store the prepared matza in a plastic bag or plastic wrap for up to four days in the refrigerator.

*

You may reuse your paper towels to wet matza, depending on how strong they are. Adhere to the approximated drying times for both processes of the matza in order to allow for the Al-Dente, firm but not to soft texture. At this point you should not have any problems using the matza sheets for our recipes or yours...

...Enjoy!

Layering Method

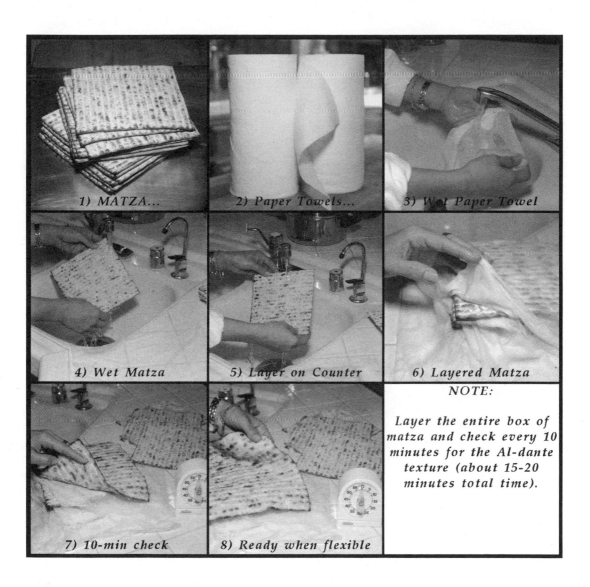

1) MATZA...

2) Paper Towels...

3) Wet Paper Towel

4) Wet Matza

5) Layer on Counter

6) Layered Matza

7) 10-min check

8) Ready when flexible

NOTE:

Layer the entire box of matza and check every 10 minutes for the Al-dante texture (about 15-20 minutes total time).

Recipe Value Info...

Now that we are well into our third edition and have toured throughout the country, we have learned some of the needs and wants requested by our various audiences. One of the most commonly asked questions during our workshops is, what are the various fat and caloric values for each recipe. You can substitute various items to bring down the fat and caloric values, and we provide you with some suggestions.

Cooking light by altering an ingredient of the original recipe will slightly change the taste of a recipe. Using butter or margarine definitely adds a richer flavor to Matza 101's recipes. These traditional recipes were designed to have full-bodied flavor, whether an entree or dessert. The idea back in our Grandmother's day was not to change or alter the original ingredients, but to eat what tastes good and to cut back what you eat in half (hence, lowering fat and calorie content). So, instead of having a full "dollop", you'll have half a "dollop". Today in the 90's, there have been so many great developments in various foods, (i.e. fat and calorie content) that it makes life a little bit easier with controlling the foods that we eat -- which in some cases may have to compensate for the taste.

We felt it would be a great addition to have some alternatives with various ingredients, such as lowfat and light foods. You will notice that some of the ingredients have enclosed brackets ( ) with an asterisks * inside. This gives you an option to have the recipe as originally set up or you can substitute the ingredients to reflect a low fat recipe.

NOTE: When purchasing lowfat cheeses, be sure to strain overnight because of the high water content. This will insure the proper consistency for our recipes. Although egg whites can be substituted for whole eggs, you can still lower the fat value by using half the amount of eggs suggested and supplementing with egg whites.

Should you require nutritional value information in reference to the individual recipes, you can obtain a separate pamphlet with further details from Matza 101. You may reach us at (909) 483-3902 or E:mail to matza101@AOL.com.

Matza Scraps

SWEET GRANOLA: Again, while on tour and workshops, we brought matza granola for our audience to sample! The granola was made with leftover matza from our sweet recipes. Remember, the matza is already flavored with orange juice, vanilla sugar and margarine.

Simply take the scraps, raw slices of almond, and generously sprinkle with some additional sugar and cinnamon; mix well and scatter onto a 9 x 13 cookie sheet; bake in a 350 degree oven until crisp. We suggest if you are going to use 4 cups of scraps, then add 1 cup of almonds. During the process of cooking, you will need to toss and separate scraps to loosen. Separate the scraps every 15 to 20 minutes; this will allow the granola to evenly cook and crisp; remove from oven and let cool.

You can now flavor further by melting chocolate chips and drizzling over the now MATZA GRANOLA; place in the freezer for about 45 minutes; remove and start breaking into bite size granola. The granola will store well in an airtight bag or container for up to 2 months.

SAVORY GRANOLA: When making the savory recipes... remember, the matza is already flavored with margarine, garlic powder, onion powder, salt and pepper.

Gather the savory scraps, place onto a 9 x 13 cookie sheet and bake in a 350 degree oven until crisp. Toss every 20 minutes. You can add other savory flavors such as parmesan cheese, sesame seeds, paprika, Cheyenne pepper, etc...

Remove from the oven and serve as soup or salad toppers, or as a snack... Store in an airtight bag or container for up to 2 months.

SO, REMEMBER, KEEP THOSE SCRAPS!!!

ENJOY!

"Matza Facts"

Why does this book differ from all other books? With this book we have only matza recipes; why with this book do we eat only matza?"

Because Matza is the bread of affliction used for Passover, and we have created 101 recipes for you to try this Passover holiday. The most important symbol for Passover is eating unleavened bread called matza.

Matza Facts

In the days of the Talmud, the perforation of the matza was artistic and the little holes in the matza were shaped as figures, animals, and flowers. The perforating was done with a tool that looked like a comb. Later in years, the perforation tool was a wheel. Today we know the shape of matza as either round or square; during the Middle Ages matza was shaped even triangular.

About the later 1800's, matza-baking machinery was invented in England. Soon after, it was introduced in America. Although some matza (Matza Shemurah - guarded matza) are still made by hand, most Passover matza today are made by machine. Actually, matza is used all year round.

It is noted that the Lubavitch Rebbe ate matza not only on Passover, but on Shabbat and holidays throughout the year.

It is recorded that a large portion (over 30%) of the American population is allergic to yeast products and for dietary purposes use matza throughout the year. Matza is also a wheat product and is free of fats and sugars. Unlike other countries, the U.S. is fortunate to have the availability of matza throughout the year.

Matza 101 - Unique recipes for eating at the Seder and celebrating true freedom throughout the Passover Holiday...

ENJOY!

Fish... Kugels... Casseroles... Dairy...

Matza Cheese Lasagna

Preheat Oven 350 Degrees - Preparation Time 30 Minutes - Yield 8

This is one of our favorite and easy to make recipe. This is "the" recipe that gave us the reason to begin writing MATZA 101!   The best part is you will use the matza strait out of the box. You will prepare the tomato sauce first, and while that cooks up a delicious storm, you can prepare the filling.   We will gather the following ingredients for the SAUCE...

2	*Tablespoons Oil (*Vegetable Cooking Spray)*
2	*Medium Onions, Finely Chopped*
1	*Celery Stalk, Finely Chopped*
6	*Garlic Cloves, Pressed*
4	*Cups Peeled Tomatoes (Fresh, Or Canned With Juice)*
4	*Cups Tomato Sauce*
1/2	*Cup Tomato Paste*
1	*Cup Water*
2	*Tablespoons Of Lemon Juice, Fresh*
1	*Tablespoon EACH Basil And Oregano, Fresh Or Dried*
	Salt And Pepper To Taste (Suggest 1 Tblsp Pepper)

Heat oil over medium heat for about 30 seconds; add onion and celery. Sauté until limp and the onion is light brown. Add garlic; sauté for about 30 seconds. Lower heat; add the remaining ingredients and let the sauce cook uncovered for about 15 minutes, stirring occasionally.   Remove from heat and leave sauce uncovered. While the sauce cooks up, prepare the FILLING...

6	*Sheets Of Matza (Used For Layering)*
2	*Cups Cottage Cheese (*Lowfat)*
2	*Cups Ricotta Cheese (*Lowfat)*
2 1/2	*Cups Grated Mozzarella Cheese (*Skim Milk/Lowfat)*
1	*Cup Grated Parmesan Cheese (*Light)*
1	*Egg, Beaten (*2 Egg Whites)*
1/8	*Teaspoon Nutmeg (If Available For Passover)*
1	*Teaspoon Black Pepper*
1/4	*Cup Chopped Fresh Parsley*

Reserve 1/2 cup of the mozzarella cheese and 1/2 cup of the parmesan cheese. Mix all of the above ingredients in a bowl, with the exception of the matza. Grease a 9 x 13 x 2 deep dish pan and place some of the tomato mixture in the bottom. Place two pieces of matza over the sauce, side by side, and top the matza with 1/3 cup of the cheese mixture, and top with some (1 cup) of the sauce. Repeat the layering and end with the tomato sauce. Top with reserved mozzarella cheese and parmesan cheese. Place in preheated oven for about 45 minutes. Let cool for about 15 minutes and serve with extra sauce on the side...ENJOY!

Matza Eggplant Lasagna

Preheat Oven 350 Degrees - Preparation Time 30 Minutes - Yield 8

The eggplant preparation in this recipe is unique in that you won't fry the eggplant. It is simply roasted and used as part of the layering process. Again, a basic sauce will be used in order to bring out the distinct flavor of the eggplant. Lets begin by making the SAUCE...

1	*Tablespoon Oil (*Vegetable Cooking Spray)*
2 1/2	*Cups Mushrooms (Fresh Or Canned)*
4-5	*Cloves Of Garlic, Pressed*
1	*Teaspoon Dried Basil*
1/2	*Teaspoon Dried Oregano*
1/2	*Teaspoon Coarse Black Pepper*
4	*Cups Crushed Tomatoes (Including Juices)*
1/4	*Cup Water*

Heat oil in a medium sized skillet over medium heat. Add the mushrooms and sauté for about 5 minutes. Add the garlic and sauté for about 30 seconds. Add the remaining ingredients; cover, reduce heat to <u>medium-low</u> and simmer for about 30 minutes. While the sauce cooks up, gather the remaining ingredients...

1	*Large Eggplant, Peeled And Sliced Lengthwise*
1	*Cup Parmesan Cheese, Grated (*Light)*
2	*Cups Ricotta Cheese*
1	*Egg, Beaten*
1/4	*Cup Parsley, Finely Chopped*
3/4	*Cup Mozzarella Cheese (For Topping -*Skim Milk/Lowfat)*
4	*Sheets Of Matza*

Place eggplant slices, single layer onto greased cookie sheet. Place in preheated oven and bake for about 15 minutes. Turn eggplant over and bake for an additional 15 minutes. Remove from oven, let cool and cut up into about 1/2" pieces. In a medium sized mixing bowl, or in food processor, combine 1/2 cup parmesan cheese, ricotta cheese, egg and parsley; mix well.

Grease an 11 x 8 baking dish. Place some of the tomato mixture on the bottom. Place 2 pieces of matza over the sauce, and top the matza with half of the cheese mixture, half of the sliced eggplant, and half of sauce. Repeat the layering and end with the tomato sauce. Top with mozzarella cheese and 1/2 cup parmesan cheese. Place in preheated oven for about 45 minutes. Let cool for about 15 minutes before serving...ENJOY!

Matza Gefilte Fish Enchiladas
Preheat Oven 350 Degrees - Preparation Time 30 Minutes - Yield 24

Many of us find ourselves with left-over Gefilte Fish. For a change and different taste that is sure to please any Gefilte Fish lover, try this new recipe. *You can use any poached or grilled fish and even substitute the fish for chilies or cheese.* The jalapeno sauce we have created is beyond words of "simply delicious". You will need the following ingredients for the FISH ENCHILADAS...

6	*Prepared Matza*
6	*Gefilte Fish Pieces (1 Jar, Rinsed And Drained)*

Grease two 13 x 9 casserole pans with margarine. Cut prepared matza into fourths, set aside. Cut each Gefilte Fish ball into fourths and place one fourth of fish ball onto one fourth of prepared matza, roll up and place seam side down onto casserole pans. To prepare the JALAPENO SAUCE you will need...

2	*Tablespoons Butter (*Vegetable Cooking Spray)*
1	*Onion, Chopped*
4	*Jalapeno Chilies , Seeded And Minced (Fresh Or Canned)*
2	*Cloves Garlic, Pressed*
1/2	*Teaspoon Cayenne Pepper (If Available For Passover)*
1/2	*Teaspoon Cumin (If Available For Passover)*
1/2	*Teaspoon Chili Powder (If Available For Passover)*
1/2	*Teaspoon EACH Black Pepper And Salt, Or To Taste*
1	*Cup Cream (*Whole Milk)*
1	*Cup Sour Cream (*Light Sour Cream)*
1/4	*Cup Milk (If Necessary To Thin Sauce)*
4	*Cups Jack Cheese, Shredded (*Light - 1 1/2 Cup For Top)*
1	*EACH Red And Yellow Pepper, Roasted, Peeled And Diced*

> For Matza Cutting see Diagram 2

In a medium sized skillet, melt the butter and sauté the onion, add the chilies, garlic, and spices; add the cream and lower heat to a simmer until thickened, about 15 minutes. Add the sour cream and if you feel that it's necessary to thin the sauce, then add the milk. Simmer for an additional 2 minutes and finally add 2 1/2 cups of cheese and stir until cheese melts. Pour the sauce over rolled Gefilte Fish and sprinkle with remaining cheese. Place casseroles in preheated oven for about 25 to 30 minutes or until cheese has lightly browned. Garnish with roasted peppers. Serve with a green salad and fresh vegetables...ENJOY!

Matza `N` Cheese Casserole

Preheat Oven 350 Degrees - Preparation Time 30 Minutes - Yield 20

This mock macaroni and cheese casserole made with matza as the substitution for noodles, is not only an easy dish to prepare, but incorporates two of our favorite cheeses with a rich creamy mushroom sauce. Served with a salad and our Matza New York Style Cheese Cake as dessert, WOW, what a meal! If you are in a hurry or pressed for time, then simply break the dry matza into pieces instead of preparing the matza. So, let's begin by preheating the oven to 350 degrees, and gather the following ingredients for your CASSEROLE...

> For Matza
> Cutting see
> Diagram 3

12	*Prepared Matza*
5 1/2	*Cups Cream Of Mushroom Soup (*Canned With Water)*
4	*Cups Cheddar Cheese, Grated (*Light)*
4	*Cups Jack Cheese, Grated (*Light)*
8	*Tablespoons Margarine (*Vegetable Cooking Spray)*
	Tablespoon Black Pepper

First you will grease a 14 1/2 " x 10" glass baking dish with 1 tablespoon margarine. Cut the prepared Matza into 1/2" strips, resembling extra wide egg noodles and set aside. Reserve 1 cup of each grated cheese to top casserole before baking.

Thoroughly mix cream of mushroom soup, cheese, and pepper in a large mixing bowl. Then, fold in the Matza strips. Pour mixture into your baking dish and dot with remaining margarine and sprinkle 2 cups of mixed cheeses on top of casserole.

Bake casserole in preheated oven for about 1 1/2 hours or until browned. Serve hot out of the oven, and compliment with a tossed green salad and fruit... ENJOY!

NOTE: When using lowfat recipe eliminate margarine and coat the pan with vegetable cooking spray.

Matza Potato Knishes

Preheat Oven 400 Degrees - Preparation Time 30 Minutes - Yield 16

Either the beef or potato knish will do in satisfying any taste bud... either one is easy. We found that it was so simple to prepare knishes that we made both, potato and meat, at the same time and even mixed the potato mixture with the meat mixture as a stuffing. This, of course, is just another good alternative. Again, the same rule will hold in baking savory dishes, in that you can alternate powdered spices for fresh. OKAY, enough jabbering, lets get the POTATO KNISH stuffing by gathering the following ingredients...

4	Cups Water
2	Tablespoons Instant Chicken Soup Mix (Parve)
1	Teaspoon Black Pepper
2	Cups Mashed Potatoes (3 Large Potatoes)
2	Large Onions, Finely Chopped
2	Eggs, Beaten (*4 Egg Whites)
	Salt To Taste

In medium sauce pan mix 4 cups water, instant chicken soup mix, pepper and bring to a boil. Add potatoes and cook thoroughly. Drain, mash, and set aside to cool. To avoid extra work, use the same sauce pan, and over medium heat, sauté onions in oil until well browned, and set aside to cool. When both mixtures have thoroughly cooled, in separate bowl combine the potatoes, onions, eggs, salt and pepper. Mix well and set aside. Now let's prepare the KNISH SHELLS...

16	Prepared Matza
8	Tblsp Margarine, Softened (*Light)
1/2	Teaspoon EACH, Garlic Powder, Onion Powder, Parsley, Paprika, Salt And Black Pepper
1/4	Cup Sesame Seed And Poppy Seeds (If Avail For Passover)

Grease 13 x 9 cookie sheet. In a small mixing bowl combine softened margarine with garlic powder, onion powder, parsley, paprika, salt, pepper, and seed combo. Cut prepared matza to 5" rounds (typical cereal bowl size). Brush margarine and spice mixture on both sides of matza rounds.

Place approximately two tablespoons of potato mixture in center of matza round and be sure not to overfill, as matza will crack while cooking. Fold matza round in half forming a half moon shape. Press lightly around edge to seal knish. Repeat this process until all shells are filled with potato mixture. Place knishes on cookie sheet and bake in preheated oven until browned and crisp, about one hour...ENJOY.

Matza Veggie Calzones

Roasting the vegetables and combining them with the feta cheese make for a fantastic and unique calzone. You can replace the vegetables for parboiled broccoli flowerettes or spinach, but since we have plenty of spinach recipes, we thought you would enjoy these VEGGIE CALZONES...

8	*Prepared Matza*
4	*Tablespoons Margarine, Softened (*Light)*
3	*Cups Peeled Eggplant, Chopped*
1	*Large Onion, Chopped*
1	*Cup Mushrooms, Sliced*
1	*Cup Zucchini, Chopped*
	Salt And Pepper To Taste

In mixing bowl, combine and mix eggplant, onion, mushrooms, zucchini, salt (easy on the salt, as the FETA Cheese will fill that void) and pepper. Spread onto large greased baking pan. Bake in preheated oven for about 45 minutes, stirring occasionally; remove from oven and let cool. When cooled, place veggies in bowl and mix together with the next three ingredients...

1 1/2	*Cups Feta Cheese (*Light)*
1/4	*Cup Fresh Basil, Chopped*
1	*Cup Mozzarella Cheese, Shredded (*Skim Milk Or Light)*
1/2	*Teaspoon EACH Garlic Powder And Onion Powder To Top*

Set the bowl of mixed veggies and cheese aside, and let's prepare the matza. Cut 8 prepared matza into 6-7" rounds, an average cereal bowl size. Lightly coat both sides with softened margarine. Stuff calzones with about 2 large tablespoons of the filling onto half of each circle. Fold the matza over the filling, shaping into a half moon. Place the Veggie Calzones onto cookie sheet. Top by sprinkling garlic and onion powder. Bake in preheated oven for about 20-25 minutes. Serve warm...ENJOY!

Matza Asparagus Crispers

Preheat Oven 450 Degrees - Preparation Time 20 Minutes - Yield 24

This one is for you Althea!!! We suggest grilling Halibut topped with toasted almonds, and serve crispers on the side. Althea is our vegetarian friend and health NUT. So for all of our vegetarian friends out there, give these VEGETABLE CRISPERS a try...

> For Matza Cutting see Diagram 14

6	*Prepared Matza*
3	*Tablespoons Margarine, Softened (*;Oght)*
1/4	*Teaspoon EACH Garlic And Onion Powder, Salt & Pepper, Sesame Seeds (If Available For Passover)*

Grease a 13 x 9 non-stick cookie sheet with margarine. In a small mixing bowl combine softened margarine with garlic powder, onion powder, salt, pepper, and sesame seeds. Now, take one piece of matza, brush both sides with spiced/margarine mixture, do the same for all matza and set aside. Okay, that's done. We'll now prepare ASPARAGUS STUFFING...

48	*Fresh Asparagus Tops, About 2 Pounds, Cut 3"*
2	*Tblsp Butter Or Margarine (*Vegetable Cooking Spray)*
2	*Cloves Garlic, Pressed*

Wash asparagus and break off each spear as far down as it snaps easily. In a large, non-stick skillet, sauté asparagus tips and pressed garlic in butter or margarine over medium heat just until asparagus turns light green in color, about 1 minute or so... BE CAREFUL TO NOT OVER SAUTÉ. Take prepared matza and cut into fourths. Place two asparagus tips into one matza square and roll diagonally away from you, we suggest that you begin the rolling procedure with the untrimmed edge first to give a nice finished appearance. Be sure to let asparagus tips peak through at both ends. Place the crispers seam side down onto greased cookie sheet and bake in preheated hot oven for about 10 minutes or until matza crispers are golden in color. Now, for a light SAUCE TOPPING...

4	*Cups Sliced Mushrooms*
8	*Tablespoons Butter (*Margarine Light)*
2	*Cloves Garlic, Pressed*
1	*Tablespoon Parsley, Finely Chopped*
	Salt And Pepper To Taste

In medium sized non stick skillet, melt the butter, and sauté mushrooms until browned. Add garlic, parsley, salt, pepper and continue to sauté for one minute longer. Remove the crispers from the oven, and flip seam side up, lightly top with sautéed mushroom sauce...ENJOY!

Matza Egg Folds

Preheat Oven 400 Degrees - Preparation Time 30 Minutes - Yield 48

Matza Folds? Yes, it is an unusual name, it is definitely unique because we will use leftover eggs from Passover. Folds are filled with a delicate egg/feta combination, topped with a delicious Parmesan cheese sauce, complimented by a hint of garlic and garnished with green onions. Let's gather the following ingredients for these delectable MATZA EGG FOLDS...

12	Prepared Matza
8	Tablespoons Margarine, Softened (*Light)
10	Hard-Boiled Eggs, Crumbled
1/2	Cup <u>EACH</u> Feta Cheese And Cottage Cheese (*Light)
1/4	Cup Parsley, Chopped
4	Garlic Cloves, Pressed
1	Teaspoon Pepper

> For Matza Cutting see Diagram 16

In medium sized mixing bowl mix eggs, feta cheese (crumbled), cottage cheese, parsley, garlic and pepper; mix well and set aside. Very lightly grease two non-stick cookie sheets and set aside. Trim all four sides of prepared matza as close to the edge as possible.   With a pastry brush or butter knife, lightly coat both sides of matza with margarine, then carefully cut matza into fourths.

Place about one teaspoon of egg mixture on bottom center corner of each square and gently fold matza over filling, diagonally, to form a triangle and press enough to seal edges. Make sure not to overfill. Place egg folds on cookie sheet and bake in preheated oven for about 35 to 40 minutes or until golden brown. While FOLDS are baking let's prepare PARMESAN CHEESE SAUCE...

4	Tablespoons Butter (*Magarine Light)
4	Tablespoons Matza Meal
2	Cups Heated Cream Or Whole Milk (*Whole Milk)
2	Garlic Cloves, Pressed
3/4	Cup Parmesan Cheese (*Light)
3/4	Cup Green Onion, Thinly Sliced, For Topping

In a medium sized sauce pan, melt butter over low heat. Mix matza meal into the melted butter with a wooden spoon; cook slowly, stirring all the time, for about two to three minutes or until well blended. <u>**Gradually**</u> stir in the heated cream or milk and continue to stir until mixture has thickened. Then add garlic and <u>**one tablespoon at a time**</u> of Parmesan cheese; simmer for about three minutes. Season to taste with salt and pepper. If your sauce becomes to thick, then add a little extra milk, a tablespoon at a time, until thinned to the right consistency. Place folds on serving dish, top with Parmesan Cheese Sauce and garnish with green onions...ENJOY!

Matza Stuffers, Italian Style

Preheat Oven 400 Degrees - Preparation Time 20 Minutes - Yields 14

It's MATZABLE! Stuffers are great topped with our own Marinara Sauce. We suggest simply serving with a tossed green salad for a dinner meal or lunch. Ingredients needed for SAUCE...

1	*Tablespoon Oil (*Vegetable Cooking Spray)*
1	*Medium Onion, Finely Chopped*
1/2	*Celery Stalk, Finely Chopped*
3	*Large Garlic Cloves, Pressed*
2	*Cups Peeled Tomatoes With Juice (Fresh Or Canned)*
2	*Cups Tomato Sauce*
1/2	*Cup Water*
1/4	*Cup Tomato Paste*
1	*Tablespoon Freshly Squeezed Lemon Juice*
1	*Teaspoon EACH Basil And Oregano (Fresh Or Dried)*
1	*Teaspoon Pepper And Salt To Taste*

In medium size sauce pan, over medium heat, for about 30 seconds, heat the oil and add the onion. Sauté the onion, add celery and sauté until limp and light brown, about 5 minutes. Add the garlic and sauté for about 30 seconds. Lower the heat and add the remaining ingredients, let sauce cook for about 15 minutes uncovered on medium/low heat, stirring occasionally. Remove from heat and leave uncovered. Now, let's gather the following ingredients for fantastic STUFFERS...

7	*Prepared Matza*
2	*Cups Cottage Cheese (*Light)*
1	*Egg, Room Temperature (*2 Egg Whites)*
1/2	*Cup Swiss Cheese, Grated (*Light)*
2	*Tablespoons Parmesan Cheese (*Light)*
1	*Clove Garlic, Pressed And Fresh Ground Pepper To Taste*

Grease 13 x 9 x 2 baking dish; set aside. In medium sized mixing bowl, combine cottage cheese, egg, Swiss cheese, parmesan cheese, garlic, black pepper; mix well, and set aside. Cut matza in half, *FOLLOWING THE GRAIN*. Place one heaping tablespoon of cheese mixture on one end of matza and roll it up. Place each stuffed matza seam side down onto greased baking dish, cover with about two cups of Marinara sauce, top with parmesan cheese, and bake in preheated oven for about 20 minutes. Serve with leftover Marinara Sauce on the side...ENJOY!

Matza Lasagna Spinach Rolls

Preheat Oven 350 Degrees - Preparation Time 30 Minutes - Yield 27

Unlike our traditional Matza Lasagna recipe, this recipe will require some preparation and cutting. It is well suited to please any vegetarian's pallet. You can use the tomato sauce in the Matza Lasagna recipe, or simply give this one a try for a lighter flavor. You will need the following ingredients for LASAGNA SPINACH ROLLS...

9	*Prepared Matza*
4	*Tablespoons Margarine, Softened (*Light)*
1 1/2	*Cups Grated Parmesan Cheese (*Light)*
1 1/4	*Cups Shredded Mozzarella Cheese*
2	*Cups Ricotta Cheese (*Light)*
2	*Cups Fresh Spinach, Chopped Or Frozen And Pressed*

Trim TOP and BOTTOM of prepared matza as close to the edge by following the grain for a nice finish. Now make strips by cutting matza into THIRDS, again following the grain, and set aside.

Coat two 11 x 7 baking dishes with "No Stick Cooking Spray". Drain and thaw out the spinach. In a large mixing bowl, combine 3/4 cup Parmesan cheese, all of the mozzarella cheese, ricotta cheese and spinach and stir well. Very lightly spread softened margarine on matza lasagna strips, then spread about one tablespoon, maybe less, of the spinach mixture on each strip and roll up. Arrange cut side down in greased baking dish and set aside.

1 1/2	*Cups Chopped Tomato, Fresh Or Canned*
4	*Cups Tomato Sauce*
1	*Teaspoon Each Oregano And Basil*
1/2	*Teaspoon EACH Garlic Powder And Onion Powder*
1/4	*Teaspoon EACH Salt And Pepper*
	Fresh Basil For Garnish (Optional)

The sauce is simple in that you don't have to cook it separately. You will simply mix all of the above ingredients in mixing bowl and stir well. Now, merely spoon tomato mixture over lasagna rolls. Cover and bake in preheated oven for about 45 minutes. Uncover, and top with the remaining Parmesan cheese and bake for an additional 15 minutes. Parmesan cheese burns quickly and may leave a bitter taste, therefore it is a good idea to wait until the end and melt it into the casserole to take advantage of its full bodied flavor. Garnish with fresh basil leaves, and serve with your favorite salad. This may be served as a meal, or an appetizer. This is a very filling dish for any Passover meal and a salad will truly suffice...ENJOY!

Matza Broccoli Cheese Casserole

Preheat Oven 350 Degrees - Preparation Time 15 Minutes - Yield 8

For a light vegetable casserole, try this, especially with the broccoli. We had fun with this in that it was easy to put together and it came out delicious. You can use either fresh broccoli or frozen, but we preferred fresh. If you are going to use fresh, parboil broccoli for about five minutes and be sure not to overcook. This was one of our quick 2:00 AM creative recipes and we are sure you will be pleased. Let's get cooking, by gathering the following ingredients for BROCCOLI CHEESE CASSEROLE...

4 1/2	*Cups Broccoli Flowerettes, Parboiled*
1	*Cup Sour Cream (*Light)*
1	*Cup Cottage Cheese (*Light)*
4	*Tablespoons Margarine, Melted (*Eliminate)*
2	*Eggs (*4 Egg Whites)*
1	*Cup Hand Cracked Matza*
1	*Large Tomato, Thinly Sliced*
1/2	*Cup Grated Parmesan Or Romano Cheese (*Light)*

Lightly grease 11 x 8 baking dish. Spread broccoli flowerettes in dish. In medium size mixing bowl, beat sour cream, cottage cheese, margarine and eggs until well blended. Fold in cracked matza and pour mixture over broccoli. Arrange tomato slices on top and sprinkle with parmesan cheese. Bake in preheated oven for about 45 minutes.

Be sure to let casserole cool for about five minutes before serving. You may serve with creamed soup and salad... Told you it was easy, ENJOY!

*NOTE: For *light cooking, use vegetable cooking spray to coat the pan.

Matza Cannelloni

Prosper, my husband enjoyed making cannelloni -- he did a great job and managed to keep the kitchen clean. This is simply delicious, no room to talk, trust us, tease the entire family with CANNELLONI- we will begin with the sauce first...

1/4	*Cup Oil (*Vegetable Cooking Spray)*
1	*Large Onion, Finely Chopped*
3	*Garlic Cloves, Pressed*
3	*Cups Tomato Sauce*
3	*Tablespoons Tomato Paste*
1	*Teaspoon Basil*
1	*Teaspoon EACH Salt And Black Pepper*

In a medium sized sauce pan, heat the oil, add the onion and sauté until golden, then add the garlic and sauté for about 30 seconds longer.   Add tomato sauce and paste, basil, salt, pepper; let sauce cook at medium heat for about 15 minutes. While this cooks up, let's make the WHITE SAUCE...

4	*Tablespoons EACH Butter And Matza Meal (*Light)*
2	*Cups Heated Cream (*Whole Milk)*
2	*Garlic Cloves, Pressed*
3/4	*Cup Parmesan Cheese (*Light)*

In a medium sized heavy-bottomed sauce pan, melt butter over low heat. Mix matza meal into the melted butter with a wooden spoon; cook slowly, stirring all the time, for about two to three minutes or until well blended. **Gradually** stir in the heated cream and continue to stir until mixture has thickened. Then add garlic, and **one tablespoon at a time** of Parmesan cheese; simmer for about three minutes. Season to taste with salt and pepper. If your sauce becomes thick, then add extra cream, a tablespoon at a time, until thinned to the right consistency.
Now, for CANNELLONI..

7	*Prepared Matza*
1	*Egg (*2 Egg Whites)*
1	*Cup EACH Cottage Cheese And Ricotta Cheese (*Light)*
2	*Tablespoons EACH Parsley, Chopped & Parmesan Cheese*
1/2	*Teaspoon EACH Salt And Pepper*

Grease 13 x 9 x 2 baking dish. In medium bowl, combine above ingredients (NOT MATZA), mix well. Cut matza in half, *FOLLOWING THE GRAIN* . Place 1 tablespoon of mixture on one end of matza and roll it up. First place white sauce on bottom of baking dish, then add stuffed matza seam side down, finally top with red sauce, and bake in preheated oven for 30 minutes...ENJOY!

Matza Chili Pepper Rellenos

Preheat Oven 350 Degrees - Preparation Time 30 Minutes - Yield 8

A very easy toss-it-together Spanish casserole any family will love. It can be made to be spicy depending on the chili peppers you will use. Serve this simply with a salad, matza tortilla chips and our salsa recipe. During the rest of the year, you can easily serve chili rellenos with beans and rice. You will need the following ingredients for CHILI PEPPER RELLENOS...

4	**Sheets Of Matzas**
6-8	**Whole Green Chili Peppers (Canned Or Roasted)**
1	**Cup Shredded Cheddar Cheese (*Light)**
1	**Cup Shredded Monterey Jack Cheese (*Light)**
4	**Eggs, Beaten (*8 Egg Whites)**
1 1/2	**Cups Milk (*1% Lowfat)**
2	**Tablespoons Matza Meal**
1/2	**Teaspoon EACH, Salt, Garlic Powder, Black Pepper, Cumin (If Available For Passover)**
1	**Tablespoon Fresh Parsley**
	Paprika And Sliced Green Onion For Garnish

Grease a 4 x 8 baking dish. Rinse chili peppers and pat dry with paper towel. Cut the peppers in half length-wise to remove the seeds. Place 2 matzas on the bottom of baking dish, place half of the chili peppers on top of matza. Sprinkle with half of both cheeses. Repeat process with remaining matza, chilies, and cheese. In separate mixing bowl, combine eggs, milk, matza meal, salt, garlic powder, black pepper, cumin, and parsley; beat with a wire whisk until smooth. Pour over casserole and bake uncovered in preheated oven for about 35 minutes or until egg mixture is thoroughly set.

Garnish by sprinkling paprika and sliced green onions. You will find this serves well with sour cream and salsa...ENJOY!

Matza Vegetable Cheese Quesadilla

Stove Top - Preparation Time 10 Minutes - Yield 48

This recipe worked out well with all of our children... It was quick and simple, and they enjoyed watching us make these quesadillas as well as eat them. Quesadillas are traditionally from Mexico are round flour tortillas are used. Using matza served as a good and easy alternative. Serve the quesadillas with sour cream, salsa and avocados on the side, a tossed green salad, and our Matza Chips. Basically, it is a very versatile recipe in which the matza can be filled to your liking. One option to go with for QUESADILLAS is as follows...

12	*Prepared Matza*
4	*Tblsp Margarine (For Browning Or *Vgtbl Cooking Spray)*
2	*Cups Jack Cheese, Shredded (*Light)*
2	*Cups Cheddar Cheese, Shredded (*Light)*
2	*Large Tomatoes, Thinly Sliced*
4	*Long Green Onions, Thinly Sliced*
2	*Long Green Peppers, Thinly Sliced*
1/2	*Teaspoon <u>EACH</u> Garlic Powder, Onion Powder, Black Pepper*

Place large sized non-stick skillet over medium heat, dot with enough margarine to evenly coat pan. Now place one prepared matza in the skillet and moderately arrange by sprinkling the cheese first, followed by sliced tomatoes, green onions, green peppers, and finally remaining spices. Be conservative in layering your ingredients because you will do the same for the remaining five quesadillas. Once you have layered each matza, then cover the filling with another matza and let ingredients melt. Now, turn over filled matza so that the other side will cook up to a crisp making QUESADILLAS. Do the same for all quesadillas to follow.

Once the quesadillas have cooked and you have removed them from the pan, be sure to let cool a bit before cutting into wedges. Each matza will be cut up into 8 pieces. First, cut matza in half horizontally, then cut in half vertically, and finally cut diagonally left and then right, yielding 8 wedges per quesadilla...ENJOY!

Matza Asparagus Swiss Quiche

Preheat Oven 350 Degrees - Preparation Time 15 Minutes - Yield 8

Quiches in general sound complicated but are so simple to make, especially with handling the matza as a basis for crust.   All quiches amount to, is a simple custard with whatever fillings you desire. Gather the following ingredients and try some of our fancier favorites, which include our ASPARAGUS SWISS QUICHE...

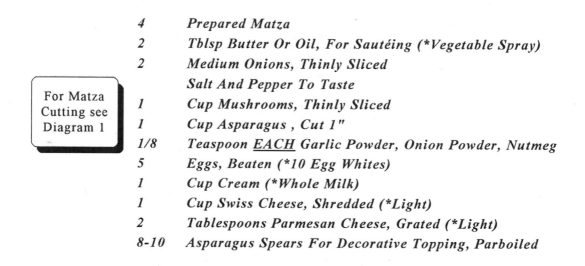

4	*Prepared Matza*
2	*Tblsp Butter Or Oil, For Sautéing (*Vegetable Spray)*
2	*Medium Onions, Thinly Sliced*
	Salt And Pepper To Taste
1	*Cup Mushrooms, Thinly Sliced*
1	*Cup Asparagus , Cut 1"*
1/8	*Teaspoon <u>EACH</u> Garlic Powder, Onion Powder, Nutmeg*
5	*Eggs, Beaten (*10 Egg Whites)*
1	*Cup Cream (*Whole Milk)*
1	*Cup Swiss Cheese, Shredded (*Light)*
2	*Tablespoons Parmesan Cheese, Grated (*Light)*
8-10	*Asparagus Spears For Decorative Topping, Parboiled*

For Matza Cutting see Diagram 1

Grease 9" pie pan with margarine.   Place four prepared matza in front of you so that they are arranged to form a square. Turn your pie pan upside down over arranged matza squares. With a sharp knife cut around pie pan leaving a one inch border. You should have four matza wedges forming a circle. Now, turn pie pan right side up and place wedges with points at center of pan, so that pan is covered forming a matza crust.

In medium sized skillet, melt butter over medium heat and sauté onions for about three minutes. Then add mushrooms, salt, pepper, and sauté for two more minutes. Finally, add asparagus pieces, garlic powder, onion powder and sauté for two more minutes. Let cool and set aside.

In medium sized mixing bowl combine eggs, cream, nutmeg, parmesan cheese and set aside. Place asparagus/onion mixture on bottom of matza pie pan. Add one cup of shredded Swiss cheese on top and finally, add cream mixture.

Place quiche in preheated oven for about 35 to 45 minutes. Check for doneness by placing a knife or toothpick in center of quiche, if it comes out clean, then quiche is done. Remove quiche from oven, let cool and decorate by arranging parboiled (30 to 45 seconds) asparagus spears resembling a wheel...ENJOY!

Matza Broccoli Quiche

Preheat Oven 350 Degrees - Preparation Time 15 Minutes - Yield 8

Delicate broccoli flowerettes swirled around in a delicate blend of cheeses, encased in a thin crispy matza crust... Well, who could ask for anything more! Cooked to perfection, this quiche may be served as an entree with a green salad and fruit or cut into smaller pieces and can be served as an appetizer. Our BROCCOLI QUICHE, as well as our other quiches, are not only simple to make but are just as beautiful in their presentation...

4	*Prepared Matza*
4	*Tablespoons Margarine, Softened (*Light)*
3	*Cups Broccoli Flowerettes*
1 1/2	*Cups Medium Carrots, Shredded*
1	*Medium Onion, Chopped*
10	*Eggs PLUS 1 Cup Milk (*14 Egg Whites)*
1/2	*Cup Parmesan Cheese, Grated (*Light)*
1/2	*Cup Mozzarella Cheese, Shredded (*Light)*
1/2	*Cup Monterey Jack Cheese, Shredded *Light)*
1/4	*Cup Cheddar Cheese, Shredded (*Light)*
11 /2	*Teaspoon Pepper*
1	*Teaspoon EACH Salt, Garlic Powder, Onion Powder*

For Matza Cutting see Diagram 1

Grease 9" pie pan. Using a butter knife coat one side of each matza with softened margarine and sprinkle with half garlic/onion powder. Place four prepared matza in front of you, buttered side up, so that they are arranged to form a square. Turn your pie pan upside down over arranged matza squares. With a sharp knife cut around pie pan leaving a one inch border. You should have four matza wedges forming a circle. Now, turn pie pan right side up and place wedges, (coated side) with points at center of pan, so that pan is covered forming a matza crust. Lightly coat prepared matza inside pan with margarine, sprinkle with remaining garlic/onion powder.

In medium sized skillet, melt 1 tablespoon margarine over medium heat and sauté onions and carrots for about three minutes. Let cool and set aside.

In medium sized mixing bowl, combine broccoli, eggs, milk, cheeses, salt, pepper, and cooled onions and carrots. Mix well and pour this mixture into prepared quiche pan. You can sprinkle parmesan cheese on top. Place quiche in preheated oven for about 45 minutes. Check for doneness by placing a knife or a toothpick in center of quiche, and if comes out clean, then the quiche is done. Let cool...ENJOY!

Matza Spinach Quiche

Preheat Oven 350 Degrees - Preparation Time 15 Minutes - Yield 8

Spinach, in general, goes well with feta cheese. This combination is a wonderful delight that will surely please the pallet. You will find that any quiche serves well with salad and fruit. Let's gather the following ingredients for a light SPINACH QUICHE...

4	*Prepared Matza*
2 1/2	*Cups Cooked Drained Spinach, Stems Removed, Chopped*
1/8	*Teaspoon Nutmeg (If Available For Passover)*
1	*Tablespoon Lemon Juice*
2	*Tablespoon Parsley, Chopped*
1	*Teaspoon Black Pepper*
1	*Cup Feta Cheese, Crumbled (*Light)*
4	*Eggs, Beaten (*8 Egg Whites)*
3/4	*Cup Heavy Cream (*Whole Milk)*
1/2	*Cup Plain Yogurt (*Lowfat)*

For Matza
Cutting see
Diagram 1

Grease a 9" pie pan.   Place four prepared matza in front of you so that they are arranged to form a square. Turn your pie pan upside down over arranged matza squares. With a sharp knife cut around pie pan leaving a one inch border. You should have four matza wedges forming a circle. Now, turn pie pan right side up and place wedges with points at center of pan, so that pan is covered forming a matza crust.

In medium sized bowl, mix spinach, nutmeg, lemon juice, parsley, pepper, and spread this mixture on the bottom of matza crust. Gently place feta cheese on top of spinach mixture. In a bowl beat eggs, cream, yogurt and blend well; pour over spinach mixture.

Place quiche in preheated oven for about 40 to 45 minutes. Check for doneness by placing a knife or toothpick in center of quiche, if it comes out clean, then quiche is done...ENJOY!

Matza Banana Blintzes

Stove Top - Preparation Time 20 Minutes - Yield 24

Besides the traditional cheese stuffed blintzes, there are various ways of serving blintzes which includes stuffing them with fresh fruit or fruit preserves. In this recipe we will use fresh firm ripe bananas to stuff the prepared matza and prepare a wonderful caramelized sauce for topping the blintz. It is suggested to serve these immediately off the skillet, and we found that the BANANA BLINTZES serve well with cottage cheese and fresh fruit on the side...

6	*Prepared Matza*
3	*Tablespoons Margarine, Softened (*Light)*
1/4	*Cup Orange Juice*
1	*Teaspoon Vanilla*
1/4	*Cup Sugar*

For Matza Cutting see Diagram 2

Cut prepared matza into fourths and if you choose, you may also trim edges of matza. You will find it easy to combine orange juice and vanilla in a small spray bottle. Spray orange juice/vanilla mixture on both sides of prepared matza and set aside. With a pastry brush or butter knife spread softened margarine on both sides of prepared matza and sprinkle both sides with sugar.

6	*Firm Bananas*
1/4	*Cup Lemon Zest, Grated*
1/2	*Cup Sweet Kosher Wine*
4	*Tablespoons Butter*
4	*Tablespoons Sugar*
1/4	*Cup Orange Juice*
1/4	*Cup Orange Zest, Grated*

Now, slice your bananas in half lengthwise and then slice in half again, basically slicing the bananas into fourths. Arrange one quarter of a banana on each matza square, sprinkle each one with lemon zest and about 1/2 teaspoon sweet wine, and roll up.

In a large sized skillet over medium heat, melt three tablespoons of the sugar until it becomes a liquid, amber in color, and bubbly, basically until sugar has caramelized. Add one tablespoon of the wine and 2 tablepsoons butter, and constantly mix until liquid is well blended into the caramelized sugar. Now add 1/8 cup orange juice, lemon/orange zest and mix.

Arrange half of the banana filled blintzes in the skillet, seam side down, (about 6 at a time) and spoon the sauce over them. After the bottom side browns, gently roll each blintz over, add some kosher wine and sprinkle the blintzes with about 1/4 tablespoon of sugar. Finally, you will briefly brown the opposite side and constantly shake the pan; repeat. Serve immediately and...ENJOY!

Matza Caramel Pears Al-Dente

Stove Top - Preparation Time 20 Minutes - Yield 12

Did you think that you could savor a delicious crepe during Passover? Well you can, especially the way in which we prepare the matza ahead of time. Our pear/caramel crepe will definitely melt in your mouth. These matza crepes are cooked to a delicate crisp and can be served as a wonderful after dinner dessert, or as a mouth savoring breakfast. For PEARS AL-DENTE you'll need...

For Matza Cutting see Diagram 15	

6	*Prepared Matza*
3	*Tablespoons Margarine, Softened (*Light)*
1/4	*Cup Orange Juice*
1	*Teaspoon Vanilla*
1/4	*Cup Sugar*

Grease a large non-stick skillet and set aside. Combine orange juice and vanilla in small spray bottle. Take prepared matza and spray both sides with orange juice/vanilla mixture. You can set matza aside to allow for better saturation, about 1/2 hour. Using a butter knife or pastry brush, coat both sides of matza with softened margarine and generously sprinkle both sides of matza with sugar and set aside. Now, we will prepare the FILLING...

3	*Pears, Thinly Sliced (Fresh)*
4	*Tablespoons Butter (For Browning)*
1/2	*Cup Brown Sugar, Firmly Packed*
1/3	*Cup Water*
1/2	*Teaspoon Lemon Peel, Grated*
1/3	*Cup Cream Cheese (3 Oz Package) (*Light)*
1	*Tablespoon Vanilla*
1	*Tablespoon Sugar*
1/3	*Cup Sliced Almonds, Toasted*

In a small sauce pan combine brown sugar, water, and lemon peel. Heat until boiling or until sugar dissolves; reduce heat to keep warm. In a small mixing bowl, combine cream cheese, vanilla, sugar, and blend until smooth. Stir in almonds, *reserving one tablespoon.* Now, take one piece of matza, *PLACING MATZA GRAIN VERTICALLY IN FRONT OF YOU*, and carefully spread cream cheese mixture onto matza crepes, about 3/4 inch from edges. Place 2-3 pear slices in the lower center of matza. Fold lower part of matza over pears, then fold over both sides, and finally roll up firmly. Place crepes in a buttered skillet seam side down. Repeat this process being sure not to over crowd crepes while browning. Once all crepes are in skillet, increase the heat level to medium. When crepes are well browned on the bottom, gently turn over and pour caramel sauce over crepes. Serve warm, and garnish with remaining sliced almonds...ENJOY!

Matza Cheese Blintzes

Range Top - Preparation Time 20 Minutes - Yield 12

You don't have to be Jewish to enjoy this CLASSIC. Instead of Matza Brie, try this great change and make your Passover breakfast a delight by topping blintzes with sour cream and serve with fresh fruit. Experiment, and try replacing cheese filling with blueberry or apple pie filling, or even combine the cheese and pie filling. *BE SURE NOT TO OVERFILL.* You will need the following ingredients for CHEESE BLINTZES...

For Matza Cutting see Diagram 6	

12	*Prepared Matza*
3/4	*Cups Orange Juice*
1	*Tablespoon Vanilla And 1/3 Cup Sugar*
8	*Tablespoons Margarine, Softened (*Light)*

Cut prepared matza into 6" rounds (average cereal bowl size). You will find it easy to combine orange juice and vanilla in a small spray bottle. First, spray orange juice/vanilla mixture on both sides of prepared matza. Next, coat prepared matza rounds with softened margarine on both sides and sprinkle with sugar. Let's prepare the BLINTZ FILLING by gathering the following ingredients...

2	*Cups Hoop Or Farmer Cheese (Alternate With Ricotta Or Cottage Cheese Drained Through A Cheese Cloth) (*Dry Curd, Uncreamed)*
1	*Large Egg (*2 Egg Whites)*
6	*Tablespoons Sugar*
1/2	*Teaspoon Vanilla*
1/8	*Teaspoon Salt*
4	*Tblsp Butter Or *Cooking Spray (For Browning Blintzes)*

In medium size mixing bowl, combine above ingredients (except for butter or margarine), mix well and set aside. Place two tablespoons of butter or margarine in a large size, non-stick skillet, over low heat allowing margarine to melt throughout pan.

Place matza so that the grain is vertically in front of you. Place one tablespoon of cheese filling on lower center of matza round, fold lower part over cheese, then fold over both sides, and finally roll up firmly. Place blintz in skillet seam side down. Repeat this process until you have four to six blintzes in your skillet. Be sure not to over crowd blintzes while browning; otherwise, blintzes will be difficult to turn when crowded. Once all blintzes are in skillet you can increase the heat level to medium. When blintzes are well browned on the bottom, gently turn over to allow browning on the other side until golden.   Repeat this process with remaining six blintzes. Serve warm with sour cream and fresh fruit... ENJOY!

Matza Fruit Kugel

Preheat Oven 350 Degrees - Preparation Time 20 Minutes - Yield 16

Being that Passover is in the spring time, you'll find this fruit kugel a different and refreshing delight. So let's try this Matza Custard KUGEL made extra special with fruit and spices...

8	*Prepared Matza*
1/2	*Cup Orange Juice*
1	*Teaspoon Vanilla*
1/2	*Cup Sugar*
4	*Tablespoons Margarine, Softened (*Omit)*

Lightly grease 13 x 9 x 2 baking dish with either butter or margarine and sprinkle with some of the sugar. Combine orange juice and vanilla in a small spray bottle. Take prepared matza and spray both sides with orange juice/vanilla mixture. For better saturation, set matza aside for 1/2 hour. Using a pastry brush or butter knife, brush both sides of matza with margarine and sprinkle both sides with sugar. Now for the FILLING, you will need...

3	*16 Ounce Cans Fruit Cocktail, Drained (*Light Syrup)*
6	*Large Eggs (*10 Egg Whites)*
2/3	*Cup Sugar*
2	*Cups Sour Cream (*Light)*
1/2	*Teaspoon Cinnamon*
2	*Teaspoons Vanilla*

In medium sized mixing bowl beat eggs until light and fluffy. Add the sugar, sour cream, cinnamon, vanilla and beat until well mixed. Stir in drained fruit cocktail and set aside. Arrange two prepared matzas side -by-side into prepared pan. Spoon about two thirds of fruit mixture over matza. Add another layer of matza. Repeat this layering ending with fruit mixture. Place in preheated oven for about one hour or until the top of the kugel has risen and is golden. Finally, for the TOPPING...

2	*Cups Whipping Cream (*Light)*
2	*Tablespoons Powdered Sugar*
1/2	*Cup Almonds, Sliced And Toasted*

In a small mixing bowl, combine the whipping cream and sugar and whip until the cream has formed stiff peaks. Serve KUGEL warm and place on individual servings about one heaping tablespoonful of whipped cream and garnish with sliced almonds. There is no way you'll hear a boohoo in the house...ENJOY!

NOTE: Use vegetable cooking spray to coat the pan to avoid sticking.

Matza Sweet Kugel

Do Ahead Recipe - Preheat Oven 350 Degrees - Preparation Time 20 Minutes Yield 16

A real simple and delicious dessert to please the family on Pesach or any Shabbat.   This is a very simple "DO AHEAD" type of recipe. It is required that you refrigerate the Matza KUGEL overnight or at least 3 hours prior to cooking. Preparation time is about 20 minutes, and it is suggested to prepare KUGEL in the morning. You will need to use a 9 x 13 glass baking dish.

Prepare the Matza, and trim the edges of the Matza to save for topping the KUGEL at the end. We found that some brands of Matza crackers have burnt edges, and we treated this by cutting the edges and saving them for a fantastic cinnamon/sugar topping. *Be sure to cut the edges and set aside for TOPPING.* You will need the following ingredients for the KUGEL...

> For Matza
> Cutting see
> Diagram 3

12	*Prepared Matza (Cut Into 1/2" Strips)*
7	*Eggs (*10 Egg Whites)*
1	*Cup Sugar*
2	*Cups Cottage Cheese (*Light)*
1 1/2	*Teaspoon Vanilla*
1	*Cup White Raisins*
3	*Cups Milk (*1% Lowfat)*
8	*Tablespoons Melted Butter Or Margarine (*Omit)*
2	*Cups Sour Cream (*Light)*

Beat the eggs well, then thoroughly mix all of the ingredients except for the prepared matza and raisins. Now that all is mixed, fold in the Matza and the raisins. Pour mixture into 9 x 13 glass baking dish, cover with a plastic wrap, and refrigerate overnight or at least 3 hours. You will find that the consistency will be loose before refrigeration, but it will set when chilled.

When you are ready to bake, preheat your oven to 350 degrees. Prepare the TOPPING, which will require the following ingredients...

2	*Cups Reserved Matza Edges (Cut Into 1/2" Strips)*
1/4	*Cup Vanilla*
2	*Tablespoons Sugar*
1	*Teaspoon Cinnamon*
4	*Tablespoons Butter/Margarine (*Omit)*

Mix the vanilla, sugar, and cinnamon until the sugar granules are dissolved. Fold in Matza, and let soak for about 15 minutes. Meanwhile, dot the KUGEL with butter or margarine. Evenly distribute the matza edges on the KUGEL (sprinkle with separate mixture of 2 tblsp. sugar plus 1/4 tsp. cinnamon) and bake in preheated oven for about 1 1/2 hours or until golden brown on top...ENJOY!

NOTE: Use vegetable cooking spray to coat the pan to prevent sticking.

Matza Fruit Pancakes

Stove Top - Preparation Time 15 Minutes - Yield 12

This is one fantastic and delicious way of using up your matza scraps leftover from prepared matza used in our various recipes. These fruit matza pancakes take almost no time to prepare and serve well for Breakfast. Delight the family by serving FRUIT PANCAKES with sour cream and powdered sugar to garnish...

2	Cups Matza Scraps (Full And Compacted Cups)
1	Cup Milk (*Lowfat)
4	Eggs, Beaten (*6 Egg Whites)
2	Cups Fruit, Diced (Apples, Pears, Peaches, Etc.)
2	Tablespoons Sugar
4	Tablespoons Margarine (*Light)
1 1/2	Cups Sour Cream (*Light)
1/4	Cup Powdered Sugar

In a large bowl, break matza scraps into pieces and combine with the milk until liquid has been absorbed. Add the eggs, fruit, sugar, and mix well.

Over medium heat, place about two tablespoons of margarine in a medium sized non-stick skillet. It is real important that skillet is properly heated before starting to cook pancakes. Now, place about 1/3 cup of the fruit/matza mixture in the hot skillet. Spread the mixture with the back of the spoon to somewhat flatten out pancake to about 3 to 4 inches wide. This will allow room for about 3 pancakes in your skillet at a time. Cook for about three minutes on each side or until golden, then transfer onto a serving platter, garnish with sour cream and powdered sugar and...ENJOY!

Matza Savory Pancakes

Stove Top - Preparation Time 15 Minutes - Yield 12

These savory pancakes use up your leftover matza scraps and transforms an ordinary meal into a delicious accompaniment for any type of soup or salad. You can also serve savory pancakes with meat dishes by substituting Parve Instant Clear Soup Mix for your liquid instead of milk. The variations for these pancakes are endless... So, use your imagination and give this quick and economical dish a try. Let's begin by gathering the following ingredients for SAVORY PANCAKES...

2	*Cups Matza Scraps (Full And Compacted Cups)*
1	*Cup Milk Or Liquefy Any Parve Flavored Instant Soup Mix*
4	*Eggs, Beaten (*8 Egg Whites)*
1	*Cup Minced Green Scallions Or Long Green Onions*
2	*Garlic Cloves, Pressed*
1	*Tablespoon Parsley, Finely Chopped*
1	*Teaspoon Freshly Ground Black Pepper*
1/2	*Teaspoon Salt*
1/3	*(Approximately) Cup Oil Or Margarine For Cooking Pancakes (*Vegetable Cooking Spray)*

In a large mixing bowl, break matza scraps into pieces and combine with the milk until liquid has been absorbed. Add the eggs, scallions, garlic, parsley, black pepper, salt and mix well.

Over medium heat, place about two tablespoons of margarine in a medium sized non-stick skillet. It is real important that skillet is properly heated before starting to cook pancakes. Now, place about 1/3 cup of the savory matza mixture in the hot skillet. Spread the mixture with the back of the spoon to somewhat flatten out pancakes to about 3 to 4 inches wide. This will allow room for about 3 pancakes in your skillet at a time. Cook for about three minutes on each side or until golden, then transfer onto a serving platter...ENJOY!

You can serve savory pancakes as a side dish; you can break them up and toss over salad; you can place in the bottom of a soup bowl and pour hot soup over pancakes; or, enjoy them plain as they are, hot off the skillet!

Matza Brei

Stove Top - Preparation Time 20 To 30 Minutes - Yield 8

This Pesach classic is a light traditional meal and can have many variations whether it is a sweet taste you prefer or a savory one. With this recipe, we will prepare a Sweet Matza Brei, but we also have created a Savory Matza Brei on the page to follow. After all, we need to place a good old fashioned recipe in Matza 101 every now and then. Lets gather the following ingredients for the MATZA BREI...

8	*Matza Sheets*
2	*Tblsp Butter Or Margarine (*Vegetable Cooking Spray)*
6 To 8	*Extra Large Eggs (*12 Egg Whites)*
1 1/2	*Cups Milk (*Lowfat)*
1/2	*Teaspoon Cinnamon*
1/4	*Cup Sugar*

Place a large, non-stick skillet over a low flame and melt butter or margarine, making sure you coat entire pan with butter or margarine.

While margarine or butter is melting, take a large mixing bowl and combine eggs, milk, cinnamon and sugar. Beat until well mixed, set aside. Now, take your matza and quickly run it through your tap water, making sure you wet both sides of your dry matza. Break wet matza into pieces over egg mixture and mix until matza is well coated.

Place matza/egg mixture into hot, buttered skillet, increase heat to medium and fry matza on both sides until golden brown, as if you were scrambling eggs. Serve hot and sprinkle with additional cinnamon and sugar...ENJOY!

Matza Brei Savory Style

Stove Top - Preparation Time 20 To 30 Minutes - Yield 8

This is a great savory Matza Brei recipe that can be a delicious switch from the traditionally sweet Matza Brei. So, give this savory concoction a try and see what you think. Let's gather the following ingredients for SAVORY BREI...

8	*Matza Sheets*
1	*Large Onion, Sliced Or Chopped*
1	*Cup Sliced Mushrooms, Drained And Rinsed*
2	*Tablespoons Oil (*Vegetable Cooking Spray)*
8 -10	*Extra Large Eggs (*12 Egg Whites)*
1 1/2	*Cups Milk (*Lowfat)*
	Salt And Pepper To Taste

Place a large, non-stick skillet over a low flame and sauté onion and mushrooms in oil until tender. While onions and mushrooms are sautéing, take a large mixing bowl and combine eggs and milk. Beat until well mixed and set aside.

Now, take your matza and quickly run it through your tap water, making sure you wet both sides of matza. Break matza into pieces over your egg mixture and mix until matza is well coated.

Place matza/egg mixture into hot skillet containing onions and mushrooms, increase heat to medium, add salt and pepper and fry matza on both sides until golden brown, as if you were scrambling eggs...ENJOY!

Matza Salmon Carousels

Preheat Oven 425 Degrees - Preparation Time 30 Minutes - Yield 12

These salmon rolls make for a fantastic casserole that can be served for dinner with a tossed green salad and steamed vegetables. The combination in rolling these and placing them into a casserole has earned this dish its title. If you enjoy Gefilte Fish, then you are in for a treat with SALMON CAROUSELS...

6	*Prepared Matza*
1	*Tablespoon Oil (*Vegetable Cooking Spray)*
1	*Medium Onion, Chopped*
1	*Carrot, Grated*
1	*Celery Stalk, Chopped*

In a hot small sized skillet add oil and sauté the above ingredients, with the exception of the matza. It should take about 5 minutes; set aside. In food processor combine the sautéed vegetables along with the following ingredients and process for about 2 minutes; set aside.

1 1/2	*Cups Pink Salmon (Canned 14 Oz. Or Fresh)*
1	*Egg (*2 Egg Whites)*
1/8	*Cup Matza Meal*
1/2	*Teaspoon Salt*
1/4	*Teaspoon Garlic Powder*
1/4	*Teaspoon Crushed Black Pepper*
1/8	*Teaspoon Nutmeg (If Available For Passover)*

Now we will prepare a quick sauce that will go over the carousels. In a sauce pan combine...

2	*Cups Tomato Sauce*
5	*Cloves Garlic, Pressed*
1	*Long Green Pepper, Finely Sliced*
1	*Teaspoon Paprika*
1/2	*Teaspoon Oil (*Vegetable Cooking Spray)*
	Salt And Pepper To Taste

Grease an 8 x 11 casserole pan; set aside. Simmer the above ingredients for about 10 - 15 minutes.   Trim the top and bottom of the matza by following the grain, then cut the matza in half, yielding 2 sheets per matza. Place 2 tablespoons of the salmon stuffing at the end of each strip, and roll against the grain. Place rolls into casserole pan seam side down. Pour sauce over the rolls and place in a preheated oven for 30 minutes. Let this cool for about 15 minutes before serving...ENJOY!

Matza Salmon Pockets

Preheat Oven 400 Degrees - Preparation Time 30 Minutes - Yield 24

Listen up Salmon Pattie Lovers... Try this delicious salmon filling in a thin layer of matza, baked to a delicate crisp, and then topped with cream of celery to make this dish simply delightful. Well, it's sure to melt in your mouth and accompanied with a tossed salad, you've got a quick and easy meal in a matter of minutes. Let's begin by gathering the following ingredients for MATZA SALMON POCKETS...

12	*Prepared Matza*
8	*Tablespoons Margarine, Softened (*Light)*
2	*Tablespoons Oil (*Vegetable Cooking Spray)*
2	*Medium Onions, Finely Chopped*
2	*Celery Stalks, Finely Chopped*
2	*Medium Carrots, Grated*
2	*Large Garlic Cloves, Pressed*
4	*Cups Canned Salmon (About 2 Cans)*
2	*Eggs, Beaten (*4 Egg Whites)*
1/4	*Teaspoon Salt*
1	*Tablespoon Black Pepper*
1/4	*Cup Parsley, Finely Chopped*
3	*Cups Cream Of Celery Soup (About 2 Cans) (*Lowfat)*

Lightly grease two baking dishes with margarine. In medium sized skillet heat oil and sauté onion, celery, and carrot until onion is browned. Add garlic and sauté for about thirty seconds and remove from heat (eliminate this step of sautéing for a crunchier taste).

In a food processor bowl, combine salmon, eggs, salt, pepper, and sautéed onion mixture. Process until consistency is pate-like, about two minutes, then fold in chopped parsley.

Trim all four sides of prepared matza as close to the edge as possible. With a pastry brush or butter knife coat both sides of matza with softened margarine, then carefully cut matza into fourths. Now, place about one heaping teaspoon of salmon filling in the center of one matza square and cover filling with another matza square, gently pressing edges to seal matza pocket. Place salmon pockets onto baking dish and bake in preheated oven for about an hour and a half or until browned. Before serving, in a small sized sauce pan, heat cream of celery and top each pocket with about one tablespoon of sauce...ENJOY! *NOTE: It is preferred that bones and skin be removed from canned salmon.*

Matza Tuna Casserole

Preheat Oven 350 Degrees - Preparation Time 30 Minutes - Yield 20

This casserole may be altered to your preference. Ranging from any type of cheese to any type of vegetable, whether it be fresh or frozen. This recipe is very versatile and can be made to perfection depending upon your own individual taste. If you are in a hurry, you'll find that dry, cracked matza works out just as well as the prepared matza. Let's begin by preheating the oven to 350 degrees, and gather the following ingredients for your CASSEROLE...

For Matza Cutting see Diagram 3	

12	*Prepared Matza*
4	*Tablespoons Margarine (*Omit)*
3	*Cups Water Packed Tuna (Rinsed And Drained)*
5	*Cups Lowfat Cream Of Celery Or Cream Of Mushroom Soup*
6	*Cups Grated Cheese (Combination Of Mozzarella, Jack, And Cheddar Cheese) *(Lowfat)*
1	*Cup Milk (*Lowfat)*
2	*Cups Frozen Petite Carrots And Onions*
1	*Tablespoon Black Pepper*

First, grease a 14 1/2 " x 10" glass baking dish. Cut the prepared Matza into 1/2 " strips, resembling extra wide egg noodles and set aside. Reserve 2 cups of mixed grated cheeses to top casserole before baking.

Thoroughly mix all ingredients, except Matza strips and margarine, in large mixing bowl. Then, fold in the Matza strips. Pour mixture into your baking dish and dot with about 2 tablespoons margarine and top with 2 cups of reserved mixed cheeses.

Bake this casserole in preheated oven for about 1 1/2 hours or until browned. Serve hot out of the oven, and compliment with a tossed green salad... ENJOY!

NOTE: Use vegetable cooking spray to prevent food from sticking.

Matza Tuna Bakes

Preheat Oven 450 Degrees - Preparation Time 20 Minutes - Yield 12

Our Tuna Bakes are another easy-to-prepare recipe, simply made with just dry matza and baked in the oven to a crisp perfection. These tuna bakes are topped with mozzarella, parmesan cheese, and sliced tomatoes. For a quick and presentable lunch, our TUNA BAKES are just the recipe for you...

3	*Sheets Of Matza (Broken Into Fourths By Your Using Your Hands)*
3	*Tablespoons Margarine, Softened (*Light)*
2	*Cups Tuna (Rinsed And Drained Thoroughly)*
1/2	*Small Onion, Chopped*
2	*Tablespoons Mayonnaise (*Light)*
1	*Teaspoon Lemon Juice*
	Salt And Pepper To Taste

Grease a 9 x 13 cookie sheet and set aside. Take your dry matza and break up into fourths. Coat both sides of matza with softened margarine, and place onto greased cookie sheet; set aside. In a medium sized mixing bowl, combine tuna, onion, mayonnaise, lemon juice, salt and pepper; mix well. Now, take your tuna mixture and spread evenly over coated matza. Gather the following ingredients for the TOPPING...

2	*Cups Mozzarella, Shredded (*Light)*
2	*Tomatoes, Thinly Sliced (*Light)*
1/4	*Cup Parmesan Cheese, Grated (*Light)*

Top tuna mixture with shredded mozzarella cheese, then arrange your tomato slices and finally, sprinkle with parmesan cheese . Bake in preheated oven for 15 minutes, let cool...ENJOY!

Matza Tuna Tostadas

Preheat Oven 400 Degrees - Preparation Time 30 Minutes - Yield 12

Try this crispy tostada shell; topped with a delicious tuna melody that is absolutely out of this world... We guarantee it will have you coming back for more!   This recipe serves well with our matza tortilla chips and salsa. Let's gather the following ingredients for TUNA TOSTADA SHELLS...

12	*Prepared Matza*
8	*Tablespoons Margarine, Softened (*Light)*
1/2	*Teaspoon EACH, Garlic Powder, Onion Powder, Salt, Pepper*

Coat two 13 x 9 cookie sheets with "No Stick Cooking Spray".   Using a sharp knife, cut prepared matza into 6" rounds (typical cereal bowl size). In a small size mixing bowl, combine softened margarine with garlic powder, onion powder, salt and pepper. Brush margarine and spice mixture on both sides of matza rounds. Place matza rounds onto cookie sheet and bake in preheated oven for about 15 to 20 minutes or until browned and crispy--depending upon your preference as to how well done you want your tostada shells. While the shells are cooling, let's prepare the TUNA TOSTADA FILLING...

1 1/2	*Cups Canned Tuna, Water Packed (Rinsed And Drained)*
2	*Cups Lettuce, Shredded*
2	*Cups Cheese, Shredded (Jack And Cheddar) (*Light)*
6	*Whole Green Onions, Finely Chopped*
1	*Stalk Celery, Finely Chopped*
2	*Medium Carrots, Shredded*
2	*Small Tomatoes, Finely Chopped*
2	*Small, Long Green Peppers, Finely Chopped*
4-5	*Tablespoons Mayonnaise (*Light)*
4	*Tablespoons Salsa (Refer To Tortilla Chip Recipe For Salsa)*
1/4	*Teaspoon Salt*
1	*Teaspoon Pepper*
1/2	*Lemon, Freshly Squeezed*

In medium sized mixing bowl, combine above ingredients, except for lettuce and cheese; mix well. Place a good sized "dollop" of tuna mixture on your crispy tostada shell, top with lettuce and cheese and bite into a wonderful combination...ENJOY!

Matza Asparagus Rolls

Preheat Oven 450 Degrees - Preparation Time 20 Minutes - Yield 20

If you like asparagus, you'll love asparagus rolled with Feta cheese and baked to a delicate crisp. These serve well as appetizers with a tossed green salad on the side. Being that asparagus is plentiful during the Passover Holiday, give this delicious vegetarian recipe a try. You will need the following ingredients for ASPARAGUS ROLLS...

20	*Asparagus, Tips Cut 3 Inches*
4	*Cups Water*
1/2	*Teaspoon Garlic Powder*
1/4	*Teaspoon UNDERLINE EACH Salt And Pepper*

In medium sized sauce pan bring water, garlic, salt and pepper to a boil. Add the asparagus and par boil for one minute. Drain immediately and set aside. In a medium sized bowl combine the following cheese filling ingredients and set aside...

3	*Cups Mozzarella Cheese, Shredded (*Light)*
2	*Tablespoons Parmesan Cheese, Grated (*Light)*
3/4	*Cup Feta Cheese, Crumbled (*Light)*
1/2	*Teaspoon Coarse Black Pepper*

Now, let's season the matza so that we may introduce the delicate flavor. You will need the following...

10	*Prepared Matza*
4	*Tablespoons Margarine, Softened (*Light)*
1	*Teaspoon Garlic Powder*
1/4	*Cup Parmesan Cheese *(Light)*
1/2	*Teaspoon Paprika*
1	*Tablespoon Dried Parsley*

Grease a 9 x 13 baking dish. Trim top and bottom edges of each matza by following the grain, then cut the matza in half. Place about one tablespoon of the cheese filling on the matza strip, add two asparagus tips and roll. Place each roll onto greased baking dish seam side down. Brush the tops of the stuffed rolls with margarine and sprinkle tops with garlic powder, parmesan cheese, paprika, and dried parsley. Place in preheated oven and bake for about 20 minutes...ENJOY!

Matza Breakfast Cinnamon Toast Popovers

Preheat Oven 400 Degrees - Preparation Time 10 Minutes Yield 6

Matza cinnamon toast! Easiest recipe yet! Our Matza Cinnamon Toast is also fat free. Unlike the other recipes for cinnamon toast, in our recipe the matza is topped with cinnamon and sugar only, not with butter or margarine. The cinnamon and sugar melts so quickly under the broiler that it spreads evenly over the matza which gives the appearance of butter without the calories but still has that great cinnamon/sugar flavor. So give this simple recipe a try, pop the MATZA CINNAMON TOAST in the broiler and instantaneously you have a quick breakfast popover before school, or a great afternoon snack...

6	*Dry Matza*
1/2	*Cup Sugar*
1	*Teaspoon Cinnamon*

Be sure to stay by the broiler, as these Popovers bake quick. We suggest that you serve these with cottage cheese and fresh fruit.

Place dry matza on aluminum foiled broiler pan and that has been lightly sprayed with non-stick vegetable spray. In a small bowl, combine cinnamon and sugar. Sprinkle cinnamon/sugar mix on tops of matza. Place in broiler for one to two minutes or until cinnamon and sugar has melted. Remove from broiler, cool...ENJOY!

Matza Breakfast Spirals

Preheat Oven 400 Degrees - Preparation Time 20 Minutes - Yield 50

Breakfast Spirals you say, what are they? No, they are not English Tea Crumpets--but they are a dessert that serves well with tea any time of the day. Spirals do require several saturation steps but are well worth the effort. So, let's gather the following ingredients for BREAKFAST SPIRALS...

10	Prepared Matza
1	Cup Orange Juice
1	Tablespoon Vanilla
8	Tablespoons Margarine, Softened (*Light)
3/4	Cup Sugar
3	Egg Whites
1/4	Cup White Wine, Dry
1	Cup Honey
4	Tablespoons Water
1/4	Cup Powdered Sugar
3/4	Cup Roasted Almonds, Finely Chopped (Optional)

Grease two 13 x 9 cookie sheets and set aside. Combine orange juice and vanilla in a small spray bottle. Take prepared matza and spray both sides with orange juice/vanilla mixture. For better saturation, set matza aside for about 1/2 hour. Trim as close to the edge as possible all four sides of prepared matza. With a butter knife or pastry brush, coat both sides of matza with softened margarine and lightly sprinkle both sides with sugar. In a small bowl, combine egg whites and wine and lightly brush both sides of matza with this mixture. Now, follow the grain of the matza and cut horizontally into fifths, yielding five 1/2" strips per matza.

Gently roll each strip into a cylinder formation and place upright onto the cookie sheet. Continue this process until your cookie sheets are filled with spirals. Place in preheated oven and bake for 35 to 40 minutes or until golden.

While Breakfast Spirals are baking in the oven, let's prepare the honey glaze. In a small sized sauce pan, combine honey and water over low heat until water has been absorbed into the honey, about five minutes. When spirals have completely cooled, lightly drizzle honey mixture over matza spirals, and finally before serving, sprinkle with powdered sugar and almonds...ENJOY!

Matza Borekas

Preheated Oven 400 Degrees - Preparation Time 30 Minutes - Yield 36

Borekas made with matza, UNHEARD OF!!! The intricacy of this recipe has been made so simple in utilizing matza, that even the novice cook will be amazed. This Middle Eastern filled pastry is an absolute must for serving either at Passover or throughout the year. It's presentation is not only inviting but spectacular enough to impress and fool anyone in believing that it could possibly be matza. Let's gather the following ingredients for Leah's favorite, BOREKAS...

18	*Prepared Matza*
12	*Tablespoons Margarine, Softened (*Light)*
1	*Cup Feta Cheese, Crumbled (*Light)*
2	*Cups Cottage Cheese (*Lowfat)*
1/2	*Cup Mozzarella Or Jack Cheese, Grated (*Light)*
1/2	*Cup Parmesan Cheese, Grated (*Light)*
1	*Cup Spinach, Finely Chopped And Compressed*
1	*Egg, Beaten (*2 Egg Whites)*
1	*Teaspoon Black Pepper*
1/2	*Cup Sesame Seeds For Topping (If Available For Passover)*

For Matza Cutting see Diagram 4

In medium sized mixing bowl, combine all cheeses, spinach, egg and black pepper; mix well and set aside.

Very lightly grease two non-stick cookie sheets and set aside. Trim all four sides of prepared matza as close to the edge as possible.   With a pastry brush or butter knife lightly coat both sides of matza with softened margarine, then carefully cut matza into fourths.

Place about one teaspoon of cheese mixture on bottom center corner of each square and fold matza over filling, diagonally, to form a triangle and press enough to seal edges. Make sure not to overfill. ***If matza cracks while folding, don't panic, it's okay, because you are going to wrap another quarter of matza over the first triangle.*** In other words, you will use two quarters for one Boreka. The first quarter will be used to fill and form the triangle, and the second quarter will be used as a cover to fold over the first triangle. Try not to directly overlap the second quarter over the first triangle. Leave a small gap to give the Boreka a somewhat leafy effect. Place Borekas onto cookie sheets until filled and generously top with sesame seeds.

Place Borekas in preheated oven for about 35 to 45 minutes or until golden. Serve with olives and pickles and...ENJOY!

Matza `N` Cheese Star Appetizers

Preheat Oven 350 Degrees - Preparation Time 20 Minutes - Yield 48

These mini Matza n' cheese stars are incredibly easy and are sure to please the cheese lover in us. If you want to make an impressionable quick appetizer, then this recipe is surely for you. You will need to use non-stick mini muffin pans to shape into star forms. The following ingredients are needed for CHEESE STAR APPETIZERS...

12	*Prepared Matza*
8	*Tablespoons Margarine, Softened (*Light)*
2 1/2	*Cups Sharp Cheddar Cheese, Grated (*Light)*
2 1/2	*Cups Monterey Jack Cheese, Grated (*Light)*
1	*Cup Sour Cream (*Lowfat)*
1	*Tablespoon Instant Powder Chicken Soup Mix (Parve)*
1/4	*Cup Green Onion, White Ends*
1/3	*Cup Sliced Ripe Olives*
1/2	*Red Pepper, Chopped*

Trim all four sides of prepared matza as close to the edge as possible. Lightly coat both sides of matza with softened margarine, then cut matza into fourths.   Gently press each quarter piece into lightly greased mini muffin cups. Place in preheated oven for about 5 minutes or until lightly browned. Remove and set aside onto greased cookie sheet. Repeat this process for more stars if necessary.

In medium sized mixing bowl combine remaining ingredients, with the exception of the softened margarine. Mix well. Now fill mini muffin matza cups with cheese filling, and bake for an additional 10 minutes or until evenly browned and crispy. Careful not to let the cheese burn.

These can easily be served directly hot out of the oven, or at room temperature...ENJOY!

Matza Cream Cheese 'N' Onion Bakes

Preheat Oven 450 Degrees - Preparation Time 10 Minutes - Yield 12

In our opinion, this savory cream cheese 'n' vegetable mousse is the best we have ever tasted. The combination of vegetables mixed into the cream cheese is just unexplainable. You will just have to prepare them and see for yourself that they will melt-in-your mouth when they come fresh out of the oven! Gather the following ingredients for CREAM CHEESE 'N' ONION BAKES...

3	Matza Sheets (Broken Up By Using Your Hands)
3	Tablespoons Margarine, Softened (*Light)
1/2	Small Carrot
1	Small Onion
1/2	Small Celery Stalk
1	Cup Of Cream Cheese, Softened (*Light)
1	Teaspoon Instant Clear Chicken Soup Mix (Parve)
1/4	Cup Parmesan Cheese (*Light)
1	Teaspoon Paprika (For Topping)

Grease a 9 x 13 cookie sheet; set aside. Take your dry matza and break into fourths, coat both sides with softened margarine, and place on to greased cookie sheet; set aside.

Food process carrot, onion, and celery until finely chopped. Add cream cheese and clear instant chicken soup mix and process until well blended.

Spread approximately two tablespoonfuls of cream cheese mixture onto coated matza, top with parmesan cheese and sprinkle with paprika. Bake in preheated oven for 15 minutes and...ENJOY!

Matza Cream Cheese Surprises

Preheat Oven 350 - Preparation Time 30 Minutes - Yield 12

Our Matza Cream Cheese Surprises are absolutely scrumptious! The surprise in this delightful dessert is a dab-ful of Apricot Jam that is placed in the center of the cream cheese filling. When my partner's husband, Prosper, bit into our Cream Cheese Surprise, his eyes lit up and he said, "Ta-eem", meaning "tasty" in Hebrew. Well, his expression was enough for us! So, this recipe became another addition to our Matza Cookbook! Let's get started by gathering the following ingredients for the MATZA CREAM CHEESE SURPRISE...

For Matza Cutting see Diagram 6	12	*Prepared Matza*
	8	*Tablespoons Margarine Or Butter, Softened (*Light)*
	3/4	*Cup Orange Juice*
	1	*Teaspoon Vanilla*
	3/4	*Cup Sugar*

Generously grease one large cookie sheet and generously sprinkle some of the sugar on to the cookie sheet. Combine orange juice and vanilla into a small spray bottle. Take prepared matza and spray both sides of matza with orange juice/vanilla mixture. For better saturation, set matza aside for 1/2 hour. Using a pastry brush or butter knife, brush or spread both sides of matza generously with margarine and sprinkle generously both sides of matza with sugar. Now, take one piece of matza and with matza grain vertically in front of you, cut with a sharp knife an approximate six inch circle, using a cereal bowl or whatever you have that comes close as a guide, set aside. Let's prepare the CREAM CHEESE FILLING...

1	*Cup Cream Cheese, Softened (*Light)*
1	*Cup Powdered Sugar*
1/4-1/2	*Cup Apricot Jam*
2/3	*Cup Granulated Sugar __PLUS__ One Teaspoon Cinnamon To Be Combined For Sprinkling On Tops Of Surprises*

In a mixing bowl, beat softened cream cheese and powdered sugar until light and fluffy, mixture will be stiff. Now, working with two pieces of matza rounds at a time and with matza grain vertically in front of you, place one tablespoon of cream cheese mixture on lower center of matza rounds. Carefully smooth and flatten cream cheese and make a well in the center of this mixture. Now place Apricot Jam in the well that you have made in the center of the cream cheese mixture. Fold lower part over cream cheese, then fold both sides in and roll away from you and firmly close. Place filled Matza Surprises on greased, sugared cookie sheet. After all your Matza Cream Cheese Surprises are on cookie sheet, sprinkle cinnamon/sugar on tops of surprises and bake in preheated oven for 40 minutes or until golden on top and bottom of Surprises. Cool completely or serve warm--your choice...ENJOY!

Matza Garlic Parmesan "Krispers"

Preheat Oven 450 Degrees - Preparation Time 15 Minutes - Yield 48

The aroma is simply wonderful while these Krispers are baking. These Krispers serve well without the accompaniment of a dip. They are very versatile whether they are served by themselves or with a delicious tossed green salad and even as a mid afternoon snack, totally your preference. Personally, we like them "one at a time", all day long--they become real addicting. If you love garlic bread you'll especially love our "KRISPERS". Give this easy recipe a try by gathering the following ingredients, and you will be eating these delightful GARLIC PARMESAN KRISPERS in no time...

6	*Prepared Matza*
4	*Tablespoons Margarine, Softened (*Light)*
1	*Tablespoon Garlic Powder*
3/4	*Cup Parmesan Cheese, Grated (*Light)*
2	*Tablespoons Dried Parsley Flakes*
1	*Teaspoon Paprika*

For Matza
Cutting see
Diagram 5

Grease a large cookie sheet with margarine. Brush one side of prepared matza, top side, with softened margarine. Sprinkle each matza with garlic powder, parmesan cheese, dried parsley flakes, and paprika.

Each matza will be cut up into eight pieces. First, cut matza in half horizontally, then cut in half vertically, and finally cut diagonally left and then right. Place un-greased side of cut wedges onto greased cookie sheet, being sure not to overlap. Place in preheated oven for about 20 minutes or until light brown...ENJOY!

Matza Garlic Teasers

Preheat Oven 400 Degrees - Preparation Time 15 Minutes - Yield 16

If you like garlic, then you are in for a treat... These go quick, so we suggest that you double up with this recipe. Lets get started with preparing GARLIC TEASERS

8	*Prepared Matza*
4	*Tablespoons Margarine, Softened (*Light)*
2	*Cups Softened Cream Cheese (*Light)*
8	*Cloves Garlic, Pressed*
1	*Celery Stalk, Chopped*
1	*Egg (*2 Egg Whites)*
1	*Cup Cottage Cheese (*Lowfat)*
1	*Teaspoon Instant Clear Soup Mix, Powder (Parve)*
1/2	*Teaspoon Coarse Black Pepper*
1	*Cup Mozzarella Cheese (For Topping) (*Light)*

Grease a large cookie sheet and set aside. Trim the top and bottom of the prepared matza by following the grain. Now, cut matza in half; again follow the grain.

In a food processor, combine the cream cheese, garlic, celery stalk, egg, cottage cheese, Instant soup mix, and black pepper; process for about 1 minute or until the mixture is creamy.

SPREAD about 2 tablespoons of the cream cheese filling on one sheet of prepared matza; roll against the grain, and place onto cookie sheet seam side down. With a butter knife or pastry brush, spread margarine on the tops and sides of Teasers. Finish by evenly spreading mozzarella cheese.

Place Garlic Teasers in preheated oven for about 30 minutes, serve and...ENJOY!

Matza Jalapeno Pockets

Preheat Oven 450 Degrees - Preparation Time 20 Minutes - Yield 24

Jalapeno pockets can be seasoned by using either hot or mild jalapeno peppers. The beauty of this recipe is that you can use either fresh or canned jalapenos. We found it simple to use canned and not deal with the roasting and peeling of the peppers. So, let's spice up our oven as well as our pallet by gathering the following ingredients for JALAPENO POCKETS...

6	*Prepared Matza*
8	*Tablespoons Margarine, Softened (*Light)*
1	*Cup Diced Jalapenos, Mild Or Hot*
4	*Garlic Cloves, Pressed*
1	*Teaspoon Oil*
1/2	*Teaspoon Salt*
1/2	*Teaspoon Pepper*
2	*Teaspoons Lemon Juice*
2	*Cups Mozzarella Cheese (*Light)*
1/2	*Cup Cream Cheese, Softened (*Light)*
1/4	*Cup Sesame Seeds (If Available For Passover)*

For Matza Cutting see Diagram 16

Trim edges of matza, then cut matza into fourths, and set aside. Grease a large cookie sheet with margarine and set aside. In a medium sized mixing bowl, combine jalapenos, garlic, oil, salt, pepper, lemon juice, mozzarella cheese and cream cheese. Use a wooden spoon to thoroughly mix and set aside.

Margarine the edges of the matza squares, then place about one tablespoon of the cheese/jalapeno filling in the center. Gently fold diagonally to form a triangle and pinch the ends together. Place onto greased cookie sheet. Using a butter knife or pastry brush, brush tops of pockets with margarine and sprinkle with sesame seeds.

Place pockets into preheated oven and bake for approximately 45 minutes. Serve jalapeno pockets with fruit as an appetizer and...ENJOY!

Matza Mozzarella Melts

Preheat Oven 400 Degrees- Preparation Time 15 Minutes - Yield 16

Another quick and easy recipe for the children to prepare either at lunch time or after school. In this case my daughter, Jessica, prepared these Matza Mozzarella Melts for a Sunday afternoon lunch. Jessica loves to be in the kitchen preparing, especially if it is a quick and easy recipe, and she doesn't have to wait too long for whatever she is preparing to get done. In any event, it is great to have the children involved in our Passover Holiday, knowing that they can prepare a variety of recipes made with matza, especially MOZZARELLA MELTS...

4	*Matza Sheets*
1 1/2	*Cups Mozzarella Cheese, Shredded (*Light)*
1	*Medium Onion, Sweet And Sliced*
1/2	*Cup Canned Mushrooms, Sliced And Drained*
1	*Medium Sized Tomato, Thinly Sliced*

Place dry matza on aluminum foiled broiler pan, that has been lightly sprayed with non-stick vegetable spray. Evenly sprinkle shredded cheese over dry matza, followed by sliced onions, then mushrooms, and finally sliced tomatoes. Place in broiler for about seven to ten minutes or until cheese has melted or in Jessica's case "I like the cheese a little brown on top, Mom"...ENJOY!

Matza Pizza Pizza Squares

Preheat Oven 450 Degrees - Prep Time 15 Minutes - Yield 10-12

Pizza is one of our favorite foods to eat, and we experimented with this recipe in many different ways. We found that this method is the easiest and tastiest way to prepare pizza. Many of you may have been preparing matza pizza in this manner for Passover yourselves.   No fancy way around this and just in case you haven't already tried, then give this method a chance. Since almost every child loves pizza, we just couldn't resist incorporating it in our book as one of our recipes. You will need the following ingredients for a zesty PIZZA SAUCE...

1 1/2	*Cups Tomato Paste*
2	*Cups Tomato Sauce*
1	*Teaspoon Basil (Dried Or Fresh)*
1/2	*Tablespoon Black Pepper*
1	*Teaspoon Lemon Juice*
1	*Onion Finely Chopped*
5	*Garlic Cloves, Pressed*
1	*Tablespoon Oil (*Vegetable Cooking Spray)*

In a medium sized bowl, mix above ingredients and set aside and prepare the MATZA PIZZA CRUST...

12	*Sheets Of Matza*
8	*Tablespoons Margarine, Softened (*Light)*
1	*Teaspoon Garlic Powder*
1	*Tablespoon Parsley Flakes*
1	*Tablespoon Parmesan Cheese (*Light)*

First, you will need to lightly grease lightly a 13 x 9 cookie sheet with "No-stick Cooking Spray".   In a small sized mixing bowl, mix together the margarine, garlic powder, parsley flakes and cheese. Now, with a pastry brush or butter knife, lightly coat both sides of matza with margarine and place matza onto the cookie sheet. Approximately four pieces should fit on one cookie sheet. Spread approximately 1/4 cup of sauce onto matza and continue this process until you have finished your sauce. Top with the following mixed cheeses and place in preheated oven for about 12 minutes...ENJOY!

4	*Cups Mozzarella Cheese, Grated (*Light)*
1	*Cup Cheddar Cheese, Grated (*Light)*

Favorite Topping (Mushrooms, Onions, Olives, Peppers, Etc...)

Matza Pizzzz-A Pockets

Preheat Oven 450 Degrees - Preparation Time 30 Minutes - Yield 10

One of these pockets makes for an ample serving. These are fantastic for a snack or if served with a salad, our pockets make a fantastic pizza lovers' meal. We'll start first by preparing a very simple tomato sauce. So, enough with "shpeal", and let's get these into the oven already. You will need the following ingredients for PIZZZZ-A POCKETS...

10	*Prepared Matza*
1 1/2	*Cups Tomato Paste*
1/4	*Teaspoon Garlic Powder*
1/4	*Teaspoon Onion Powder*
1/2	*Teaspoon Basil*
1/4	*Teaspoon Oregano*
1/2	*Teaspoon EACH Black Pepper And Salt*

For your sauce, mix the above ingredients in a medium bowl, except for the prepared matza (you never know); set aside. Trim all four sides of the matzas as close to the edge as possible and set them aside also. Gather your favorite pizza toppings or try ours...

3	*Cups Shredded Mozzarella Cheese (*Light)*
2	*Cups Canned Mushrooms, Rinsed & Drained*
1	*Cup Black Olives, Rinsed & Sliced*
1	*Cup Onions, Chopped*
1	*Cup Bell Peppers Or Green Peppers*
4	*Tablespoons Margarine, Softened (*Light)*
1/2	*Cup Parmesan Cheese (*Light)*

Grease 2 cookie sheets with margarine and set aside. On each matza square you will spread about one tablespoon tomato sauce, sprinkle some mozzarella cheese, mushrooms, black olives, onions, peppers, and a dash of parmesan cheese. Close each square diagonally, forming a triangle, and pinch ends with your fingers. Brush the tops with softened margarine and sprinkle parmesan cheese.

Place Pizzzz-a pockets in preheated oven, take a breather and enjoy the aroma. Leave pockets in the oven for about 30 minutes, remove, serve, and...ENJOY!

Matza Salsa Cream Cheese Mousse

Preheat Oven 350 Degrees - Preparation Time 20 Minutes - Yield 8

So, you ask what is "Matza Salsa Mousse"? It's simply a mousse using cream cheese as a base with salsa heated in a low temperature oven. Basically, a pie resembling a soufflé type texture and used as a party dip. As an alternate, try using small muffin pins (simply cut matza into fourths and stuff into greased muffin pins to bake with the filling. Use Matza Chips and cut up vegetables to dip into our SALSA MOUSSE...

4	*Prepared Matza*
1	*Egg, Beaten (*2 Egg Whites)*
1	*Cup Cream Cheese (8 Oz) (*Light)*
2	*Cups Sour Cream (16 Oz) (*Light)*
2	*Small Tomatoes, Finely Chopped*
1 - 2	*Jalapeno Peppers, Seeded And Finely Chopped*
2	*Tablespoons Red Onion, Finely Chopped*
1/3	*Cup Fresh Lime Juice*
1/2	*Teaspoon EACH Salt And Pepper, Or To Taste*
2	*Tablespoons Parsley, Chopped*
1/2	*Cup Cheddar Cheese, Shredded (*Light)*
3	*Long Green Onions, Thinly Sliced*

For Matza Cutting see Diagram 1

Grease a 9" pie pan. Place four prepared matza in front of you so that they are arranged to form a square. Turn your pie pan upside down over arranged matza squares. With scissors or a sharp knife cut around pie pan leaving a one inch border. You should have four matza wedges forming a circle. Now, turn pie pan right side up and place wedges with points at center of pan, so that pan is covered forming a matza crust.

In food processor blend egg, cream cheese, and sour cream for about one minute. Fold in tomatoes, peppers, onion, lime juice, salt, pepper and parsley. Pour mixture into pie pan lined with matza and bake in preheated oven for about one hour and fifteen minutes or until top browns. After mousse has cooled, top with shredded cheese and green onions...ENJOY!

Matza Spring Rolls

Preheat Oven 400 Degrees - Preparation Time 20 Minutes - Yield 48

Okay, so this is not classically Jewish but definitely delicious! Otherwise known as egg rolls, you'll find this Chinese dish with a Jewish twist simply a Vegetarian's delight. So let's chop veggies away, and gather the following ingredients for SPRING ROLLS...

12	*Prepared Matza*
2	*Tablespoons Sesame Oil (If Available For Passover) (*Vegetable Cooking Spray)*
3	*Medium Onions, Grated*
4	*Stalks Celery, Finely Sliced*
4	*Medium Carrots, Peeled And Grated*
1	*Small Cabbage, Grated (Napa Preferred)*
1	*Tablespoon Black Pepper*
2	*Teaspoons Salt*
8	*Tablespoons Margarine, Softened (*Light)*
1/4	*Cup Sesame Seeds (If Available For Passover)*

For Matza Cutting see Diagram 2

In medium size, non-stick skillet, place oil over medium heat. Simply sauté, in order, onions, celery, carrots, and cabbage for about five to ten minutes. After all vegetables have become limp, add black pepper and continue to sauté for an additional two minutes. Let cool and set aside.

Cut prepared matza into fourths (trimming all four sides of matza is optional, but not necessary). Lightly brush softened margarine on both sides of prepared matza quarters. Place about one tablespoon of cabbage mixture in lower center of matza end and roll up firmly. Place one roll at a time onto greased cookie sheet, seam side down. Repeat process until cookie sheet has been filled with spring rolls. Sprinkle sesame seeds over spring rolls and bake in preheated oven for about 30 to 40 minutes, or until golden.

When it's not Passover, you can add about 1/4 cup Soy Sauce (omit salt), after veggies are translucent. Spring rolls may be served with your favorite mustard sauce, or simply heat about 1/4 cup of your favorite jam with one tablespoon lemon juice...ENJOY!

Matza Taco Shells

Preheat Oven 400 Degrees - Preparation Time 20 Minutes - Yield 12

Would you ever think that you could prepare taco shells with matza? Wow, what a break-thru! Well, we have done just that --Tacos for any Passover night's meal. Stuffing the shells depends on your liking (fish, meat, or dairy). Serve with fruit and light salad, the making for a quick and delicious meal. During the rest of the year, you can easily serve tacos with beans and rice. You will really need cannoli tubes for this recipe which can be purchased at any kitchen shop. If you don't have the sufficient amount of tubes for twelve taco shells, you can bake four to six shells at a time and set aside for filling later. You will need the following ingredients for
TACO SHELLS...

For Matza Cutting see Diagram 7		
12	*Prepared Matza*
8	*Tablespoons Margarine, Softened (*Light)*
1/2	*Teaspoon Each, Garlic Powder, Onion Powder, Salt, Pepper*

Grease a 13 x 9 cookie sheet. Cut prepared matza to 5" rounds (typical cereal bowl size). In a small size mixing bowl, combine softened margarine with garlic powder, onion powder, salt and pepper. Brush margarine and spice mixture on both sides of matza rounds. Place two cannoli tubes inside one half of matza round, fold over, and place on sprayed cookie sheet. Fold to shape as a taco shell. The purpose for two cannoli tubes is to avoid taco shell ends from closing. Do the same for the rest of the matza rounds and place on sprayed cookie sheet. The length of this process will depend upon how many cannoli tubes you have to work with. Bake matza rounds in 400 degree oven, about 15 - 20 minutes or until lightly browned, and crispy depending upon your preference as to how well done you want your taco shells. It is not necessary to turn shells during baking...ENJOY!

NOTE: Taco shells should be cooked until crisp. If removed from oven too soon, shells will remain soft and will dry soft. If removed when crisp in oven, taco shells will remain crisp when cooled. These taco shells can be stored and will remain crisp. After completely cooled, store in airtight container.

Matza Tortilla Chips

Preheat Oven 400 Degrees - Preparation Time 15 Minutes - Yield 80 Chips

Wow! Crispy tortilla chips made out of Matza with our very own homemade salsa - what a delicious treat.   Serve simply with salsa, or be creative and place baked chips onto lightly greased cookie sheet, top with shredded cheddar cheese, thinly sliced jalapenos, and sliced green onion.   Re bake till cheese has melted and serve with sour cream and avocados on the side.   Gather the following ingredients for TORTILLA CHIPS...

10	*Prepared Matza*
8	*Tablespoon Margarine, Softened (*Light)*
1/2	*Teaspoon <u>EACH</u>, Garlic Powder, Onion Powder, Salt, Pepper*

Basically you'll need the same ingredients as in taco shells, but you will cut matza to resemble tortilla chips. In a small sized mixing bowl, combine softened margarine with garlic powder, onion powder, salt and pepper. We suggest that after you have prepared the matza, to season both sides of prepared matza with margarine mixture using a pastry brush or knife, and then cut into triangular shapes. Each matza will be cut up into 8 pieces. First, cut matza in half horizontally, then cut in half vertically, and finally cut diagonally left and then right.

Grease a couple of large cookie sheet. Place seasoned chips onto cookie sheet and *BE SURE NOT TO OVERLAP*. Bake in preheated oven for about 30 minutes or until chips are crispy. Serve with SALSA...

5	*Fresh Long Green Chilies, Finely Chopped*
5	*Medium Tomatoes, Cubed*
1/2	*Cup Parsley, Chopped*
1	*Medium White Onion, Chopped*
1	*Stalk Celery, Chopped*
3-4	*Garlic Cloves, Pressed*
1/2	*Fresh Lemon Juice, Squeezed*
1 1/2	*Tablespoon Oil*
	Salt And Pepper To Taste

For Matza Cutting see Diagram 5

In medium sized mixing bowl, combine above ingredients and mix well... You'll actually find yourself making extra chips for later snacking...ENJOY

Cooks Notes...

Meat and Poultry...

Matza Beef `N` Potato Turnovers

Preheat Oven 450 Degrees - Preparation Time 45 Minutes - Yield 48

Talk about turnovers, you'll have family and friends "turn over" in disbelief that these were made out of matza. Our turnovers were a success with both of our families, including Ron our biggest dis-believer. He loved every bite! Gather the following ingredients for delicious TURNOVERS...

12	*Prepared Matza*
4	*Tablespoons Margarine, Softened (*Light)*
1	*Tablespoon Oil (*Vegetable Cooking Spray)*
2	*Cups Onion, Chopped*
2	*Cups Canned Mushrooms, Drained And Sliced*
1	*Pound Lean Ground Beef (*Extra Lean Broiled)*
2	*Medium Potatoes, Mashed With One Tablespoon Margarine*
1/2	*Teaspoon Garlic Powder*
1/2	*Teaspoon Onion Powder*
	Salt And Pepper To Taste

For Matza Cutting see Diagram 16

Grease a large cookie sheet. In a large sized skillet, heat the oil and sauté the onions until limp. Add mushrooms, season with salt and pepper, and sauté for ten minutes. Remove from skillet and set aside. Now, place ground beef into skillet, season with salt and pepper and brown by thoroughly cooking the meat. Add the mushrooms to the browned meat and cook for about five minutes. Remove meat mixture from heat and add mashed potatoes and mix well. Season with garlic powder, onion powder, and if necessary, with salt and pepper to taste.

Cut prepared matza into fourths. Place about one tablespoon of meat mixture in the center of each quarter and fold cut side diagonally over to close and form a triangle. Place turnovers onto greased cookie sheet. Using a butter knife or pastry brush, lightly brush tops of turnovers with softened margarine.

Place turnovers into preheated oven and bake for approximately 30 minutes. Serve with olives and pickles...ENJOY!

Matza Beef Pot Pies

Preheat Oven 450 Degrees - Preparation Time 40 Minutes - Yield 10

Leftover meat lately??? Try this great recipe for any leftover meat that you may have in the refrigerator. This recipe can be cooked in advance and frozen. You will need 10 aluminum tart pans (4 1/2" x 1 1/4"). This serves well with a tossed green salad and matza croutons. So lets get our tools together and get these BEEF POT PIES going by gathering the following.

20	*Prepared Matza*
3	*Medium Diced Potatoes And 3 Large Diced Onions*
8	*Tblsp Softened Margarine (*Light) And 4 Tblsp Oil (*Vegetable Cooking Spray)*
6-8	*Cups Diced Meat (*Extra Lean Broiled)*
2	*Cloves Minced Garlic*
1	*Tblsp EACH Black Pepper, Garlic Powder, Onion Powder*
6	*Medium Diced Carrots*
1	*Stalk Celery, Diced*
1/4	*Cup Potato Starch (Consistency Preference)*
1/4	*Cup Instant Onion Soup Mix (Powder)*
8	*Cups Beef Stock*

Sauté diced onions with 2 tablespoons oil or margarine in an 8 quart sauce pan over medium heat until limp. Add beef and sauté for 2 more minutes, then add garlic, pepper, 1/2 tablespoon of each garlic powder and onion powder, and sauté for an additional minute. (Be certain not to allow the garlic to burn). Now add potatoes, carrots, and celery and simmer until potatoes are translucent, about 5 minutes. Add instant onion soup mix and use a whisk until well mixed, then add potato starch (little at a time to avoid lumping), and whisk until well dissolved. Mixture will be thick as you are mixing. Add the beef stock, whisk well and bring to boil. Simmer mixture for about 5 minutes or until thickened. (Depending upon your taste, you may want to add more potato starch for a thicker sauce. For thicker sauce use 1 tablespoon cold water to 2 tablespoon starch, mix well and add to stock).

Take 20 prepared matza and cut into 7" round pieces (average cereal bowl size). Save extra pieces for salad crouton topping. Place 10 round pieces of matza inside well greased pie tart pans. Transfer your greased matza pie crust pans onto cookie sheets (about 5 to a cookie sheet). Fill tart pans with meat /vegetable medley, be sure not to overfill. Place remaining 10 rounds to cover your tarts. Brush the matza tops with margarine, then sprinkle with onion and garlic powder. Place in 450 degree oven for about 20 minutes or until crust has lightly browned. ENJOY... For salad croutons, place matza cuttings on a well greased cookie sheet and sprinkle with onion/garlic powder, paprika, dried parsley flakes, salt. Bake in 450 degree oven until crust turns crispy.

Matza Meat Cigars

Preheat Oven 400 Degrees - Preparation Time 45 Minutes - Yield 64

These pastry filled cigars are most popular in the Middle East. They are called that because of the way they are shaped and the spicy flavor brings the smoke out of our ears. All kidding aside, we introduced this Moroccan appetizer to our friends and they absolutely loved it. You'll enjoy preparing CIGARS with matza, and although it does not entail the traditional frying, you will find our MEAT CIGARS taste just as crispy, and will bring out the smoke just the same...

16	*Prepared Matza*
8	*Tablespoons Margarine, Softened (*Light)*
1/2	*Teaspoon EACH Garlic Powder, Onion Powder & Salt*
1/4	*Teaspoon Black Pepper*

In a small mixing bowl combine the margarine, garlic powder, onion powder, salt and pepper. Trim off the edges of the prepared matza and cut each matza into fourths. Lightly coat one side of each quarter with margarine mixture; set aside, and lets gather the following for the stuffing...

5	*Cups Lean Ground Beef (2Lb.) (*Extra Lean)*
3	*Bay Leaves*
6-7	*Cloves Garlic, Pressed*
1	*Cup Parsley, Finely Chopped*
1 1/2	*Teaspoons Cumin (If Available For Passover)*
1-2	*Tablespoons Crushed Red Hot Pepper*
3	*Tablespoons Lemon*
1	*Teaspoon Salt Or To Taste*
8	*Cups Water*

In a sauce pan, place bay leaves and water and bring to a boil. Separate the meat into thirds and add into water. Cover, reduce heat and let simmer for about an hour and half; drain the juices (save 2 cups) and let the meat cool to room temperature. Place the meat and garlic in a food processor and process until the consistency is pate-like (about 2 minutes). Add the parsley and process for an additional 15 - 20 seconds. Transfer the meat mixture into a separate bowl and add the cumin, crushed red pepper, lemon, and salt; mix well with either your hands or a spoon. *OPTIONAL*: Bring reserved 2 cups of water to a boil, and now add the seasoned meat and simmer for about 10 minutes. Drain excess juices and let mixture cool.

Grease 2 large cookie sheets with margarine. Place about 1 tablespoon of the meat stuffing onto each bottom center quarter of matza; roll against the grain. Place onto cookie sheet, seam side down, coat tops with margarine. Place into preheated oven for about 35 minutes...ENJOY!

Matza Mini Franks

This is an easy to prepare "hands on " recipe and the whole family can become involved for a great Passover lunch or just a mid-afternoon snack served with fruit. So let's get started and gather the following ingredients for MINI FRANKS...

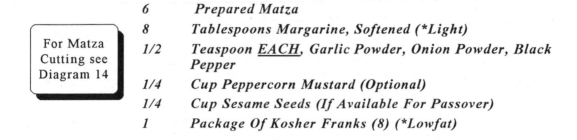

6	*Prepared Matza*
8	*Tablespoons Margarine, Softened (*Light)*
1/2	*Teaspoon EACH, Garlic Powder, Onion Powder, Black Pepper*
1/4	*Cup Peppercorn Mustard (Optional)*
1/4	*Cup Sesame Seeds (If Available For Passover)*
1	*Package Of Kosher Franks (8) (*Lowfat)*

For Matza Cutting see Diagram 14

Grease a 13 x 9 cookie sheet with "No Stick Cooking Spray". In a small mixing bowl combine softened margarine with garlic powder, onion powder, black pepper and mustard; but if you will be using peppercorn mustard, then omit black pepper in mixture.

LIGHTLY coat both sides of matza with spiced margarine mixture. Cut each frank into thirds and set aside. Cut matza in half horizontally then again in half vertically, yielding four cut pieces per matza, basically cut into fourths. Take one fourth of matza at a time and place in front of you diagonally. Place cut frank at one end of the matza and roll away from you as if you are rolling a crescent roll (diagonally) then place onto greased cookie sheet seam side down. Continue this process until all franks are rolled in matza.

Top with sprinkled sesame seeds and bake in preheated oven for about one hour. Be sure to rotate pan periodically to insure even browning. All we can say at this point is get ready to bite into a juicy frank with a deliciously light spicy flavor - Mm, Mm good! This is truly a REAL favorite with children...ENJOY!

Matza Meat Knishes

Knishes on Passover??? Oy Vey! Well, it's possible. As with all our matza dishes, the flavor you will get out of the matza depends on how it will be seasoned.   We have found in baking savory dishes that using the garlic powder/onion powder combination works well and is quick. If you wish, you can use one tablespoon each of fresh minced garlic, minced onion, and fresh finely chopped parsley. We will start by preparing the KNISH FILLING, and for this you will need...

1	*Pound Extra Lean Ground Beef (About 2 Broiled Cups)*
1	*Tablespoon Oil (*Vegetable Cooking Spray)*
1	*Large Onion, Finely Chopped*
	Salt And Pepper To Taste
1	*Egg, Beaten (*2 Egg Whites)*
2	*Cloves Garlic, Pressed*
1	*Tablespoon Matza Meal*

In large skillet over medium heat add oil and sauté onion till limp, then add ground beef and continue to brown until thoroughly cooked. Add salt and pepper to taste. Drain excess juices, if any, set aside and completely cool. In a large mixing bowl combine 2 cups cooked meat mixture, egg, garlic and matza meal. Take the mixture and run through a food processor until the consistency is pate-like (about 2 minutes). Set aside. Now lets prepare the KNISH SHELLS...

16	*Prepared Matza*
8	*Tablespoons Margarine, Softened (*Light)*
1/2	*Teaspoon EACH, Garlic Powder, Onion Powder, Parsley, Salt And Black Pepper*
1/4	*Cup Sesame Seeds (If Available For Passover)*

Grease 13 x 9 cookie sheet with "No Stick Cooking Spray".   In a small mixing bowl combine softened margarine with garlic powder, onion powder, parsley, salt, pepper and sesame seeds. Cut prepared matza to 5" rounds (typical cereal bowl size).   Brush margarine and spice mixture on both sides of matza rounds.

Place approximately two tablespoons of meat mixture in center of matza round and be sure not to overfill, as matza will crack while cooking. Fold matza round in half forming a half moon shape. Press lightly around edge to seal knish. Repeat this process until all shells are filled with meat mixture. Place knishes on cookie sheet and bake in preheated oven until browned and crisp; approximately one hour.   We guarantee that while the knishes are cooking, the aroma will get your taste buds ready to savor into a delicious crisp shell with a hearty meat and garlic flavored filling. Serve with salad and fruit...ENJOY!

Matza Chili Pepper Chicken

Preheat Oven 400 Degrees - Preparation Time 30 Minutes Yields 20

We enjoyed this recipe as it filled the kitchen with a fantastic aroma. Again, *we will be redundant* in saying that preparing the chicken was OH SO easy to make and we got thumbs up from everyone in our family - our greatest testers of all. Let's gather the following ingredients for STUFFED CHILI CHICKEN...

10	*Prepared Matza*
2	*Tablespoon Oil (*Vegetable Cooking Spray)*
4	*Cups Chicken Thighs, Boned, Skinless, Cubed (2 Pounds)*
2	*Medium Onions, Finely Chopped*
5	*Cloves Garlic, Pressed*
3	*Tablespoons Matza Meal*
4	*Teaspoons Chili Powder*
1 1/2	*Teaspoons Cumin (If Available For Passover)*
4	*Cups Chicken Broth (*Fat Free)*
3/4	*Cups Green Chili, Thinly Sliced*
2	*Tablespoons Tomato Paste*
	Salt And Pepper To Taste

In a medium sized skillet, heat the oil over medium heat for about one minute and add the chicken to cook. Stir occasionally and cook for about 7-10 minutes or until thoroughly cooked. Retain juice from the chicken and remove the chicken from skillet, place in a separate bowl and set aside.

With the juices still in the skillet, place the skillet back over heat and add the onion and garlic. Cook for about five minutes and add matza meal, chili powder, and cumin. Stir constantly and let cook for about 3 minutes. Stir in the chicken broth, chilies and tomato paste and simmer for about 5 minutes. Add the cooked chicken into the skillet and stir. Remove from heat and set aside.

Grease 13 x 9 x 2 baking pan. Cut matza in half, *FOLLOWING THE GRAIN*. Place a heaping tablespoonful of the chicken mixture on the lower part of each matza and roll it up. Place seam side down in the baking pan. Drizzle the remaining sauce over the stuffed chicken and down the center for a nice cover. Place uncovered baking pan in preheated oven for about 15 to 20 minutes. For garnish, place shredded lettuce on a platter and lay stuffed chicken on the bed of lettuce...ENJOY!

Matza Chicken Bastilla Flags

Preheat Oven 400 Degrees - Preparation Time 30 Minutes - Yield 36

Stuffed Bastilla Flags, what's that? Well, if you are familiar with the traditional Chicken Bastilla made with phyllo dough, then you will surely appreciate these appetizing flags that resemble the same flavor. If you are not familiar, then try this simply delicious pastry filled with chicken, eggs, and spices that can be served as an appetizer or as a main meal with a salad. You will need the following ingredients for CHICKEN BASTILLA FLAGS...

12	*Prepared Matza*
2	*Tablespoons Olive Oil (*Vegetable Cooking Spray)*
1/2	*Cup Medium Onion, Chopped*
2	*Garlic Cloves, Pressed*
1	*Cup Chicken, Ground-Skin Removed (About 1/2 Pound) (*Skinless, Boneless, Chicken Breast)*
1/2	*Teaspoon EACH Of Cumin, Turmeric, Cinnamon*
2 1/2	*Tablespoons Parsley, Chopped*
3/4	*Cup Chicken Stock (*Fat Free)*
1	*Teaspoon Black Pepper, Salt To Taste*
4	*Eggs, Beaten (*8 Egg Whites)*
8	*Tablespoons Margarine, Softened (*Light)*
1	*Tablespoon Powdered Sugar*

For Matza Cutting see Diagram 9

In medium sized sauce pan, heat oil, add onion, garlic and chicken. Sauté until onion is translucent. Add the cumin, turmeric, cinnamon, salt, pepper, and simmer for about five minutes. Add the parsley and the chicken stock, let simmer for about one or two minutes.

Drain the meat and save as much of the broth as possible. Place the meat into a separate bowl and set aside. Return the broth back into the sauce pan, simmer, then add beaten eggs. Stir the eggs until scrambled but not dry and add to meat mixture, mix and let cool.

Trim TOP and BOTTOM of prepared matza as close to the edge by following the grain for a nice finish. Now, make strips by cutting matza into thirds, again following the grain. Lightly spread softened margarine on both sides of strips. Place about one teaspoon of the filling on the end of each strip and fold strip away from you diagonally to the left, then fold down away from you, and finally, diagonally to the right, folding to resemble a triangle. Repeat this process until you reach the end of the strip, *SIMILAR TO FOLDING A FLAG.* Place flags seam side down onto greased cookie sheet, bake in preheated oven for 25 minutes. Let cool and sprinkle with powdered sugar, and finally...ENJOY!

Matza Chicken Bastilla

Preheat Oven 350 Degrees - Preparation Time 30 Minutes - Yield One 8

Traditionally, Bastilla is a popular Middle Eastern recipe which consists of a phyllo pie filled with chicken, almonds, sugar, and eggs. Those of us that are familiar with Bastilla will appreciate the twist in making it with matza. We have maintained the same crispy flavor for a crust, only simpler to prepare, and the combined filling puts it all together to bring you a BASTILLA made to try...

5	*Prepared Matza*
2	*Tablespoons Margarine, Softened (*Light)*
1	*Large Chicken Breast (Cooked, Skinned & Shredded)*
	Salt And Pepper To Taste
1	*Tablespoon Oil (*Vegetable Cooking Spray)*
1	*Small Onion, Chopped*
2	*Cloves Garlic, Pressed*
4	*Eggs, Beaten (*8 Egg Whites)*
1/4	*Cup Chicken Broth (*Non Fat)*
1	*Cup Almonds Finely Chopped*
2	*Tablespoons Sugar*
1/2	*Teaspoon Cinnamon*
	Powdered Sugar To Top Bastilla

For Matza Cutting see Diagram 8

In a medium sized boiling pan, boil chicken in water seasoned with salt and pepper. After the chicken has boiled, drain and save 1/4 cup of water for your broth; set aside.   Heat a frying pan over medium heat and add the oil, onion, garlic; sauté until the onion is translucent. Add the eggs, and broth and scramble until the eggs are fluffy; add salt if needed, allow to cool and set aside. In a small sized bowl combine the almonds, sugar and cinnamon. You should now have set aside your boiled chicken, scramble eggs, and almond mixture... we're almost there.

Coat an 8" pie pan with margarine. With a butter knife or pastry brush, lightly coat prepared matza with the softened margarine. Take only one piece of prepared matza, and cut into a circle; try to stay as close to the edges as possible (if you can - use pinking shears, or a ravioli cutter as this round will represent the top part of your bastilla). Place this round at the bottom of the pie pan. Now, place the other four whole prepared matzas, corners in the center, over the matza round and let them overlap your pie pan. IN ORDER, you will spread the almond mixture at the bottom of the pie, then add your seasoned eggs, and finally the shredded chicken breast. Use the overlapped pieces of matza to wrap and cover the pie.

Place your bastilla in a preheated oven, and let it bake for about 45 minutes. Remove from oven and let the pie cool for about ten minutes. *AFTER IT HAS COOLED, TURN IT UPSIDE DOWN ONTO SERVING PLATE*, and sprinkle with powdered sugar, and now...ENJOY!

Matza Chicken Pot Pies

Preheat Oven 450 Degrees - Preparation Time 40 Minutes - Yield 10

If you find yourself left with extra chicken (which we're sure most of us do), then you will find this recipe makes for a fantastic meal served with a light salad during any day of the week for Passover. This recipe can be made in advance and frozen for future use. You will need 10 aluminum tart pans (4 1/2" x 1 1/4").   NOTE: Filling can all be prepared in a sauce pan. We will begin CHICKEN POT PIES by gathering the following ingredients...

20	*Prepared Matza*
1	*Whole Chicken - Boiled Or Leftover (6-8 Cups Diced)*
8	*Tablespoons Softened Margarine Or 1/4 Cup Oil (*Light)*
2	*Medium Diced Onions*
3	*Medium Diced Potatoes*
1	*Cup Diced Celery*
2	*Cups Mixed Frozen Vegetables*
1	*Tablespoon EACH Pepper, Garlic Powder, Onion Powder*
1/2	*Cup Instant Chicken Soup Mix (Powder)*
1/4	*Cup Potato Starch*
8	*Cups Chicken Stock (Canned, Fresh, Or Water) (*Fatfree)*

Sauté diced onions with 2 tablespoons oil or margarine in an 8 quart sauce pan over medium heat until limp. Now add potatoes, celery, and frozen vegetables. Season with pepper. Simmer until potatoes are translucent. Add instant chicken soup mix and use a whisk until well mixed. Then add potato starch (little at a time to avoid lumping) and whisk until well dissolved. Don't panic, you will find the mixture thick as you are mixing. Now add the chicken, chicken stock, mix well, and bring to a boil. Simmer mixture for about 5 minutes or until thickened. *NOTE: You may have to add more potato starch to thicken mixture, depending upon your preference of consistency.* Set the thickened mixture aside to cool.

Take 20 prepared matza and cut into 7" round pieces (average cereal bowl size). Save extra pieces for salad crouton topping. Place 10 round pieces of matza inside well greased pie tart pans, or muffin tins. Transfer your greased matza pie crust pans onto cookie sheets (about 5 to a cookie sheet). Fill tart pans with chicken /vegetable medley, be sure not to overfill.   Place remaining 10 rounds to cover your tarts. Brush the matza tops with margarine, then sprinkle with onion and garlic powder. Place in 450 degree oven for about 20 minutes or until crust has lightly browned. ENJOY... For salad croutons, place matza cuttings on a well greased cookie sheet and sprinkle with onion/garlic powder, paprika, dried parsley flakes, salt. Bake in 450 degree oven until crispy...ENJOY!

Matza Tex-Mex Chicken

This one is for you if you don't like saucy foods. Try this simple union of onions and green peppers sautéed in mild spices and then stuffed with chicken into matza folds. Basically, you will find that TEX-MEX CHICKEN serves great with a tossed green salad...

8	*Prepared Matza*
4	*Tablespoons Margarine, Softened (*Light)*
1/4	*Teaspoon __EACH__ Garlic Powder, Onion Powder, Salt, Pepper*

In a small mixing bowl, combine the margarine and the dry ingredients. LIGHTLY brush both sides of matza with margarine mixture. Trim as close to the edge as possible the top and the bottom of the matza, by following the grain. Cut the trimmed matza in half, yielding 2 pieces per matza.

1	*Tablespoon Oil (*Vegetable Cooking Spray)*
1	*Medium Onion, Chopped*
2	*Long Green Mild Peppers, Finely Chopped*
3	*Chicken Breasts, Cubed (Small) (*Skinned, Boned)*
1/4	*Teaspoon Cumin (If Available For Passover)*
1/2	*Teaspoon Chili Powder (If Available For Passover)*
1/2	*Teaspoon Crushed Red Pepper*
1/4	*Cup Chicken Broth Or Water (*Fatfree)*
	Salt And Pepper To Taste

In a medium sized skillet, heat the oil and sauté the onions, and peppers for about 5 minutes. Add the chicken, and brown. Add the remaining ingredients and simmer for 10 minutes, covered.

Garlic Powder, Onion Powder, Paprika (For Topping)

Lightly grease 9 x 13 casserole pan with margarine; set aside. Place a heaping tablespoon of the chicken mixture onto one end of the matza strip and gently roll against the grain. Place Tex-Mex Chicken into casserole pan seam side down. Top by sprinkling garlic powder, onion powder and paprika. Place into preheated oven for about 35 minutes. Serve with a salad and fruit...ENJOY!

Matza Turkey Rolls

Preheat Oven 375 Degrees - Preparation Time 30 Minutes - Yield 18

These turkey rolls are great with a salad. If your in the mood for something a little different with ground turkey meat, then this one is for you. We will begin first by preparing the STUFFING...

6	*Prepared Matza*
2	*Tablespoons Margarine, Softened (*Light)*
1	*Tablespoon Oil (*Vegetable Cooking Spray)*
2	*Medium Onions, Finely Chopped*
2	*Medium Carrots, Finely Chopped*
3	*Cups Ground Turkey Meat (About 1 1/2 Pounds)(*Light)*
1/2	*Teaspoon Nutmeg (If Available For Passover)*
1/4	*Cup Parsley, Chopped*
	Salt And Pepper To Taste
1/4	*Cup Raisins*

In a medium sized skillet sauté the onions and the carrots in the oil until the onions are translucent; allow to cool. In a food processor mix the ground turkey, sautéed onions and carrots, nutmeg, parsley, salt and pepper (be sure to not include the raisins). Processes until the consistency is pate-like; about 2 minutes. Transfer this mixture into a mixing bowl and with a wooden spoon mix in the raisins.

Grease a large cookie sheet; set aside. With a butter knife, <u>LIGHTLY</u> spread margarine on both sides of prepared matza. Spread the meat filling, a heaping tablespoon, on one prepared matza and gently roll the matza against the grain. Continue with this process until you run out of filling.

Cut the prepared rolls into thirds. Place the rolls onto cookie sheet, seam side down; set aside. We will now prepare a light ORANGE GLAZE...

1	*Tablespoon Lemon Juice*
1/4	*Cup Honey*
1/2	*Cup Orange Juice (Fresh Preferred)*
2	*Tablespoons Water*

Combine the above ingredients into a small sized sauce pan and bring to medium heat. Simmer for about 5 minutes. Now, with a spoon, pour the glaze over the turkey rolls. Bake in preheated oven for about 35 minutes or until browned...ENJOY!

Desserts...

Matza Almond Cookies

Preheat Oven 400 Degrees - Preparation Time 30 Minutes - Yield 24

Almonds, almonds, almonds -- we use them even for cookies!!! These delicious chewy cookies were a definite hit with both our husbands (they can be so picky sometimes, you know what I mean)! This cookie has a chewy almond center with a delicate crispy wafer as its bottom and is garnished with sliced almonds. As with all our cookies, they are not only presentable but absolutely delicious. We hope you will enjoy our ALMOND COOKIES as much as we did...

6	*Prepared Matza*
4	*Tablespoons Margarine Or Butter, Softened (*Light)*
1/2	*Cup Orange Juice*
1/2	*Teaspoon Vanilla Extract*
1/2	*Cup Sugar*

Generously grease two large cookie sheets and sprinkle with some of the sugar. Combine orange juice and vanilla in a small spray bottle. Take prepared matza and spray both sides with orange juice/vanilla mixture. For better saturation, set matza aside for 1/2 hour. Using a pastry brush or butter knife, generously spread both sides of matza with butter and sprinkle both sides generously with sugar. Now, take one piece of prepared matza and with a round cookie cutter, three inches in diameter, cut four circles per matza, yielding 24 circles. Now, place circles onto greased and sugared cookies sheets, and we will prepare the FILLING...

1	*Cup Almond Paste*
1	*Heaping Tablespoonful Of Sugar*
1/4	*Cup Cream*
3/4	*Cup Sliced Almonds*

In a small mixing bowl combine almond paste, sugar and cream; mix until smooth. Now, take about 1/2 teaspoon of this almond mixture and place it in the center of matza round that is on your greased and sugared cookie sheet. Repeat this process until you have used up all of your almond mixture. Now, take the back of your teaspoon and run it under cool water and press back of spoon into almond mixture to spread around matza cookie. Repeat this process for all cookies. After spreading the almond mixture, take your sliced almonds and garnish each cookie. Press almond slices gently into almond paste mixture. Bake in preheated oven for 15 minutes or until lightly golden brown on top...ENJOY!

Matza Almond Squares

Stove Top - Preparation Time 20 Minutes - Yield About 24

This is a hard type of candy, almost brittle like, with a butterscotch flavor that will simply melt in your mouth. We've never tasted matza so good... As in all of our candy recipes, a candy thermometer would be beneficial to measure accurate heat level. If you don't have a candy thermometer handy, you can use the boiling point for a measure of heat as a guide, and we can help you out with this one, because it will harden rather quickly. You will need the following ingredients for ALMOND SQUARES...

1	*Cup Toasted Almonds, Chopped*
1	*Cup Matza, Hand Broken Into Bite Size Pieces*
2	*Teaspoons Salt*
2 1/4	*Cups Brown Sugar*
2 1/4	*Cups Granulated Sugar*
1 1/3	*Cups Water*
	Rainbow Confectioneries (For Topping)

In large mixing bowl, combine together almonds, matza, salt, and set aside. In a medium sized sauce pan, combine brown sugar, granulated sugar, and water. Stir over low heat until the sugar has dissolved. Place candy thermometer in sauce pan and stir over medium heat until you have reached 290 degrees. If your not using a thermometer, when the mixture reaches boiling point, keep over heat for about 5 minutes stirring mixture constantly. Remove from heat immediately and quickly add matza/almonds and stir only once or twice.

Pour the mixture into a 13 x 9 greased cookie sheet and spread thinly. As it begins to harden, mark into squares, about 1 1/2 " pieces. You will notice that this will cool rather quickly, about half an hour to one hour. When cooled, decorate by sprinkling confectioneries... ENJOY!

NOTE: To check proper heat level, you can drop a little bit of hot mixture into a separate bowl of cold water, and if the mixture forms into a hard ball, then you've GOT CANDY!!!

Matza Apple Strudel

Preheat Oven 400 Degrees - Preparation 30 Minutes - Yield 28

Apple Strudel without Phyllo dough??? Yes, without Phyllo dough! This delicious recipe is simply made with matza and is stuffed with a scrumptious apple/raisin filling and glazed with a honey/nut topping. Simplicity... Absolutely, it's at the MAX with this dessert! So, let's gather the following ingredients for the APPLE STRUDEL...

6	*Prepared Matza*
3	*Tablespoons Margarine, Softened (*Light)*
1/4	*Cup Orange Juice*
1/2	*Teaspoon Vanilla Extract*
1/4	*Cup Sugar*

Lightly grease a 13 x 9, non-stick cookie sheet and set aside. Combine orange juice and vanilla in small spray bottle. Take prepared matza and spray both sides with orange juice/vanilla mixture. You can set matza aside to allow for better saturation, about 1/2 hour. Using a butter knife or pastry brush, coat both sides of matza with softened margarine and generously sprinkle both sides of matza with sugar and set aside. Now, we will prepare the FILLING...

3	*Medium Sized Apples, Peeled And Finely Chopped*
1/2	*Cup Sugar*
1/2	*Cup Raisins*
1/2	*Cup Almonds, Finely Chopped And Toasted*
1/2	*Teaspoon Cinnamon*
1/4	*Teaspoon Nutmeg (If Available For Passover)*
3/4	*Cup Matza Meal*
1/2	*Cup Honey, For Topping*
1/2	*Cup Almonds, Toasted And Crushed -For Topping*

In medium sized mixing bowl combine apples, sugar, raisins, almonds, cinnamon, nutmeg and matza meal and set aside. Now, take one piece of matza, *PLACING MATZA GRAIN VERTICALLY IN FRONT OF YOU*, and spread three tablespoons of apple filling evenly over matza square and roll up (away from you). Place strudel onto greased cookie sheet, seam side down, repeat this process until all matza has been stuffed with apple filling. Bake in preheated oven for about 1/2 hour or until nicely browned. Remove from oven and let cool for about five minutes and then garnish by brushing the tops of strudel generously with honey and sprinkle with crushed toasted almonds. Let strudel cool completely before slicing, about twenty minutes. Mm, Mm, Good...ENJOY!

Matza Apple/Cinnamon Broilers

Preheat Oven 450 Degrees - Preparation Time 15 Minutes - Yield 8

Apples and cinnamon -- definitely a combination that compliment each other, especially with our apple/cinnamon broilers. This is a great breakfast recipe that is not only quick and easy, but is just as tasty too. Your getting a quick apple pie taste in a matter of minutes. Let's begin by gathering the following ingredients for APPLE CINNAMON BROILERS...

4	*Dry Matza*
4	*Tablespoons Margarine Or Butter, Softened (*Light)*
1/2	*Cup Sugar*
1/2	*Teaspoon Cinnamon*
1	*Apple, Thinly Sliced (Not Necessary To Peel)*
2	*Tablespoons Honey (For Drizzling On Top Of Apples Before Broiling)*

Begin by wrapping your broiler pan with aluminum foil; grease lightly with vegetable oil and set aside. In a small bowl, combine cinnamon and sugar and set aside.

Now, take your four pieces of dry matza and generously butter both sides and generously sprinkle both sides with some of the cinnamon/sugar mixture, making sure to cover entire matza. Place your coated matza onto broiler pan and arrange your sliced apples on top of matza.

Sprinkle tops of matza with some more of the cinnamon/sugar mixture and then drizzle with honey. Bake in broiler for approximately three to four minutes...ENJOY!

Matza Baklava

There is no way that you would have thought of eating the famous Baklava pastry for Passover, NO WAY! Well, guess again. Once we got the hang of manipulating Matza, there was no doubt that this wouldn't work. If you've never made Baklava, then you will be pleased with an introduction to this wonderful Greek pastry. If you're experienced, then you will appreciate the simplicity. Enough talk. Let's gather the following ingredients for the BAKLAVA FILLING...

8	*Prepared Matza*
2 1/4	*Cups EACH Almonds And Walnuts, Finely Chopped*
1/2	*Cup Sugar*
2	*Teaspoons Cinnamon*
12	*Tablespoons Butter, Melted (Or Margarine) (*Light)*

In a large mixing bowl, mix the almonds, walnuts, sugar, cinnamon and set aside. Be sure that the almonds and walnuts have been finely chopped through a food processor, about 30 seconds.

Place prepared matza on cutting board and use a rolling pin to roll out each piece as flat as possible without tearing any pieces (it's OK if some tearing occurs, because once it's cooked up, no one can tell). Trim all four sides of prepared matza as close to the edge as possible. Brush the bottom of 13 x 9 x 2 pan with some of the melted butter or margarine. Layer two pieces of matza in the pan, brush with butter. Be sure the grain of the matza is placed down the same direction at all times. Sprinkle about 1 1/2 cups of nut mixture for the first layer of filling on top of the buttered matza. Repeat second layering of matza sheets, brush with butter, add 1 1/2 cups of nut mixture. Again, layer matza sheets, brush with butter, sprinkle remaining 1 1/2 cups of nut mixture. Finally, place remaining two pieces of matza and brush the top with butter. Using a sharp knife, cut through all the layers making 18 square-shaped pieces, 3 horizontally and 6 vertically, or cut diagonally for diamond-shaped pieces. Bake in preheated oven for about 35 - 45 minutes or until golden brown. Let Baklava completely cool. Meanwhile, you will prepare the SYRUP...

1/2	*Cup EACH Honey, Sugar, Water*
1	*Cinnamon Stick*
3	*Slices EACH Lemon And Orange + 1 Tablespoon Lemon Juice*
1/2	*Teaspoon Orange Blossom Water (Optional)*

In medium size saucepan, stir together the above ingredients bringing to a boil; reduce heat. Simmer, uncovered, for about 20 minutes. Remove cinnamon, slices of orange and lemon. Immediately, while hot, generously pour all honey mixture with a spoon over top and through cracks of cooled Baklava in the pan. Cool completely, then serve... ENJOY!

Matza Banana Nut Broilers

Preheat Oven 450 Degrees - Preparation Time 15 Minutes - Yield 8

Our Matza Fruit Broilers are a great way to use up any leftover fruit. In this case we have used bananas that are topped off with toasted almonds and drizzled with honey. These broiler recipes serve well as a great breakfast treat for those "rushed" mornings. We will need the following ingredients for BANANA NUT BROILERS...

4	*Matza Sheets*
4	*Tablespoons Margarine Or Butter (*Light)*
1/2	*Cup Sugar*
1/2	*Teaspoon Cinnamon*
2	*Bananas, Sliced Diagonally*
1/4	*Cup Almonds, Toasted And Crushed*
2 - 4	*Tablespoons Honey (For Drizzling On Top Of Bananas Before Broiling*

Begin by wrapping your broiler pan with aluminum foil; lightly coat with vegetable spray and set aside. In a small bowl, combine cinnamon and sugar and set aside.

Now, take your four pieces of dry matza and generously butter or margarine both sides and generously sprinkle both sides with cinnamon/sugar mix, making sure to cover entire matza. Place your coated matza onto broiler pan and arrange your sliced bananas on top of matza.

Sprinkle tops of matza with some more of the cinnamon/sugar mixture, top with toasted almonds, and then drizzle with honey. Bake in broiler for approximately three to four minutes...ENJOY!

Matza Brown Sugar Cookies

Preheat Oven 400 Degrees - Preparation Time 30 Minutes - Yield 24

Our Brown Sugar cookies happen to be our friend, Alison's favorite cookie! She bit into this crunchy toasted almond cookie and her eyes grew as big as saucers. Saying, " Mm! I want more! She has been a reliable taster and she is beautiful as she is honest. Thank you, Alison, this BROWN SUGAR COOKIE is named for you...

6	*Prepared Matza*
4	*Tablespoons Margarine Or Butter, Softened (*Light)*
1/2	*Cup Orange Juice*
1/2	*Teaspoon Vanilla Extract*
1/2	*Cup Sugar*

Generously grease two large cookie sheets and generously sprinkle some of the sugar onto cookie sheets. Combine orange juice and vanilla in a small spray bottle and spray both sides of matza with orange juice/vanilla mixture. For better saturation, set matza aside for 1/2 hour. Using a pastry brush or butter knife, brush both sides of matza generously with margarine and sprinkle generously both sides of matza with sugar. Now, take one piece of prepared matza and with a round cookie cutter, approximately three inches in diameter, cut four circles per matza and place circles onto prepared cookie sheets. Repeat this process for all remaining matza. Bake for 15 minutes or until golden brown. ***DO NOT OVER BAKE, or MATZA ROUNDS WILL TASTE BITTER.*** Remove from oven and let cool completely before removing from cookie sheets. When completely cooled, place matza rounds on buttered rack. Now, we will prepare the BROWN SUGAR TOPPING...

1	*Cup Brown Sugar, Packed*
2	*Tablespoons Butter Or Margarine (*Light)*
3	*Tablespoons Water*
3/4 -1	*Cup Whole Toasted Almonds*

Place three, whole toasted almonds in center of matza round that is cooling on buttered rack. Heat margarine or butter, brown sugar, and water in a small sauce pan until melted. Bring this mixture to a boil and boil for about one to two minutes, stirring constantly. Remove from heat and drizzle sugar mixture over cookies topped with whole toasted almonds. Drizzle enough mixture to secure almonds to cookie. This candy topping will harden right away...ENJOY!

Matza Crystallized Nuts

This is a delicious candy bowl treat to serve with fruit and coffee. A candy thermometer would be beneficial to measure accurate heat level. If you don't have a candy thermometer handy, you can use the boiling point for a measure of heat as your guide. You will need the following ingredients for CRYSTALLIZED NUTS...

2 1/2	*Cups Packed Golden Brown Sugar*
1/2	*Cup Cream*
2	*Tablespoons Butter Or Margarine (*Light)*
1/4	*Teaspoon Salt*
2	*Teaspoons Vanilla Extract*
2	*Cups Whole Almonds Roasted*
2	*Cups Dry Matza, Bite Size Pieces*

You will need a 2 quart sauce pan to combine the sugar, cream, butter, and salt. Mix these ingredients well with a wooden spoon. Bring this mixture to a boil over medium heat. Place thermometer in mixture. Continue cooking until you reach 244 degrees (firm ball stage) stirring constantly. If your not using a thermometer, when the mixture reaches boiling point, keep over heat for about 5 minutes stirring mixture constantly.

Remove the mixture from heat and add vanilla, and fold in nuts, and matza. Continue to stir until the candy grains on the matza and nuts (the liquid will coat matza and nuts). Spread the mixture on standard, buttered cookie sheet and let cool. When candy has cooled, chip off into brittle size pieces and serve...ENJOY!

Matza Cannolies

LEIAT this one is for you. Well, what can we say, it doesn't get much easier than this for a gourmet type dessert in which a sweet shell is simply prepared with Matza and a cheese filling that is so light and fluffy. Ah! Passover has never tasted oh so good. You really need cannoli tubes for this recipe which can be purchased at any kitchen shop. It truly will be well worth the investment because this is one of the most presentable recipes and there are other recipes throughout the book that will take advantage of the cannoli tubes. If you don't have the sufficient amount of tubes for twelve cannolis, you can bake four to six shells at a time and set aside for filling later.   So lets gather the following ingredients for 12 CANNOLI SHELLS...

For Matza Cutting see Diagram 13	12	**Prepared Matza (About 1 Box)**
	3/4	**Cups Orange Juice**
	1	**Tablespoon Vanilla Extract**
	8	**Tablespoons Margarine, Softened (*Light)**
	1/2	**Cup Sugar**

Grease 13 x 9 cookie sheet with margarine and sprinkle with some of the sugar. Cut prepared matza into 5" rounds (typical cereal bowl size). You will find it easy to combine orange juice and vanilla in a small spray bottle; spray both sides of matza with orange juice mixture and allow matza to saturate for 1/2 hour. With pastry brush coat prepared matza rounds with margarine on both sides then generously sprinkle sugar on both sides. Spray cannoli tube with cooking spray and loosely wrap each matza round -- around the metal cannoli tube. Place shell seam side down onto sugared cookie sheet. Bake 15 minutes or until golden brown. The cannoli will brown and the sugar will naturally seal the seam of the cannoli shell as it bakes. After the initial 15 minutes of baking, be sure that the shell is sealed, then rotate cannoli shells to insure even browning. A total baking time of 30 minutes. Remove from heat, briefly cool enough to where you can handle the tubes to remove shells. Be sure to remove the shaped matza from the tube as soon as possible. DO NOT allow to cool to long or the shell will crack due to sugar cooling and hardening on the tube. Shells should be completely cooled before filling.
    For the most delicious filling get a grasp of the following ingredients, FILLING...

4	**Cups Ricotta Cheese (*Light)**
4	**Teaspoons Vanilla Extract**
1 1/2	**Cups Un-Sifted Powdered Sugar**
1/4	**Cup Mini Semi-Sweet Chocolate Pieces (*Reduced Fat)**
1/3	**Cup Slivered Toasted Almonds For Garnishing Ends**

Blend Ricotta in either blender or food processor until very smooth. Fold in powdered sugar and vanilla. Mix in chocolate pieces. Fill mixture into cannoli shells (pastry tube, plastic baggy or spoon). Garnish ends of cannolis with almonds, and sprinkle with sifted powdered sugar over shells.

Matza Chocolate Cherry Bars

Preheat Oven 375 Degrees - Preparation Time 45 Minutes - Yield 30

Cherries, Cherries! Yes, we do have a few recipes made with candied cherries--just because they are so pretty in their presentation, along with great color and taste. These are rich with dark chocolate flavor, layered with a delicious matza crust as the bar's base. So, give this recipe a whirl and we hope you enjoy them as much as we did...

2	*Prepared Matza*
1/4	*Cup Orange Juice*
1/4	*Teaspoon Vanilla Extract*
1/4	*Cup Sugar*

Generously grease a 13 x 9 x 2 inch baking dish and set aside. Generously grease a large cookie sheet and sprinkle some of the sugar. Combine orange juice and vanilla in a small spray bottle. Take prepared matza and spray both sides with orange juice/vanilla mixture. For better saturation, set matza aside for 1/2 hour. Using a pastry brush or butter knife, generously spread or brush both sides of matza with margarine and sprinkle generously both sides with sugar. Place on cookie sheet, bake for 15 minutes or until golden brown. Cool baked matza for about five minutes, then place in greased 13 x 9 x 2 baking dish, lining dish on bottom and approximately 1/4 inch on the sides of pan. Let cool completely, and we will prepare the DARK CHOCOLATE LAYER...

4	*Ounces Un-Sweetened Chocolate*
6	*Tablespoons Butter Or Margarine (*Light)*
2	*Cups Powdered Sugar*
2	*Teaspoons Vanilla Extract*
4-6	*Tablespoons Hot Water*

In medium sized sauce pan, heat chocolate and butter or margarine over low heat until melted; remove from heat. Stir in powdered sugar and vanilla--mixture will be stiff and lumpy until you beat in hot water, tablespoon at a time, making mixture thin enough to spread on top of matza that is layered in your baking dish. Spread chocolate over matza and put in refrigerator to cool and let set, about one hour. Now, let's prepare the TOP LAYER...

4	*Eggs (*2 Whole Eggs And 2 Egg Whites)*
1	*Cup Sugar*
2	*Cups Shredded Coconut*
1	*Cup Candied Cherries, Well Drained And Quartered*
	Powdered Sugar And Candied Cherries For Garnish

In your mixing bowl, beat eggs and sugar together until light and frothy. Carefully fold in coconut and cherries; spread over cooled and set chocolate. Bake about 20 minutes until top is FIRM to the touch. Remove from oven; let cool. Refrigerate over night. Next day, with a sharp knife, cut into desired sized bars and sprinkle with powdered sugar and garnish each bar with a whole candied cherry...ENJOY!

Matza Chocolate Chip Cookies

Preheat Oven 400 Degrees - Preparation Time 30 Minutes - 24

Our Matza Chocolate Chip Cookies are just as chewy and have a rich buttery taste that we think even gives "Famous Cookie Houses" a run for their money! These rich milk chocolate chip cookies are a great treat for any time of the day, especially in mid-afternoon when the children get home from school or they can be just as elegant served as dessert after a Passover Dinner. So let's give these MATZA CHOCOLATE CHIP COOKIES a try...

12	*Prepared Matza*
8	*Tablespoons Margarine Or Butter, Softened (*Light)*
3/4	*Cup Orange Juice*
1	*Teaspoon Vanilla Extract*
3/4	*Cup Sugar*
1	*Cup Milk Chocolate Chips (*Reduced Fat)*

Generously grease two large cookie sheets and generously sprinkle some of the sugar onto the cookie sheets. Combine orange juice and vanilla in a small spray bottle and spray both sides of matza with orange juice/vanilla mixture. For better saturation, set matza aside for 1/2 hour. Using a pastry brush or butter knife, brush or spread both sides of matza generously with margarine and generously sprinkle both sides of matza with sugar. Now, take one piece of prepared matza and with a round cookie cutter, about three inches in diameter, cut four circles per matza and place on greased and sugared cookie sheet. Repeat this cutting process with five additional prepared matza, yielding 24 matza rounds. Place matza rounds onto greased and sugared cookie sheet, set aside. Place approximately 12 to 15 milk chocolate chips in the center of matza rounds, set aside. Now, with another round cookie cutter, approximately 2 1/2 inches in diameter, cut remaining six matzas, yielding 24 smaller matza rounds. Place these smaller matza rounds on top of larger matza rounds that are on cookie sheet with chocolate chips in the center. Bake in preheated oven for 15 minutes or until golden. Remove from oven, let cool then place on buttered rack to completely cool. Let's prepare the LEMON GLAZE...

2	*Tablespoons Margarine Or Butter (*Light)*
1	*Cup Powdered Sugar*
1/2	*Teaspoon Grated Lemon Peel*
2 To 4	*Tablespoons Lemon Juice*

Heat margarine or butter in a small sauce pan until melted. Stir in powdered sugar and lemon peel. Stir in lemon juice, one tablespoon at a time, until thin. Drizzle on top of chocolate chip cookie, cool...ENJOY!

Matza Chocolate Clusters

Stove Top - Preparation Time 20 Minutes - Yield About 30

This is a semi-sweet chocolate candy that has just enough chocolate to tease the taste buds but yet satisfy them deliciously. This simple recipe is a great "hands on recipe" for children to become involved with and have fun! You will need the following ingredients for CHOCOLATE CLUSTERS...

3   *Cups Semi-Sweet Chocolate Pieces (*Reduced Fat)*
4   *Cups Matza Sheets, Hand Crumbled*
2   *Cups Salted Nuts*

In a double boiler, melt semi-sweet chocolate pieces over hot water. If you do not have a double boiler, you can place the semi-sweet chocolate pieces in a smaller sized sauce pan and place the smaller sized sauce pan into a larger sized sauce pan filled half way with water. The purpose of double boiling is to insure that the chocolate will not burn. Bring water to a boil and continue to simmer until all chocolate has melted. Another option of melting chocolate is to use your microwave. Once the chocolate has melted, set it aside and let cool at room temperature, about 15 to 20 minutes. Do not allow the chocolate to get hard.

In a greased or buttered mixing bowl, combine melted chocolate, matza, and nuts. Stir this mixture until matza is well coated with chocolate. Place a piece of waxed paper onto a 13 x 9 cookie sheet, which should be lightly coated with margarine or butter. Mixture will be sticky. With wet hands, drop tablespoonful size of matza/chocolate mixture onto cookie sheet and refrigerate for about two hours...ENJOY!

Children can mold candies with their wet hands--fun project for the entire family!

NOTE: Be brave, and experiment by adding dried fruit such as raisins, and toasted coconut.

Matza Chocolate Glazed Cookies

Preheat Oven 400 Degrees - Prep Time 30 Min. - Yield 18

These beautifully chocolate glazed matza cookies are sandwiched by a light and fluffy orange creme filling. They are rich and "one" taste may be your limit, but we dare you just to have "one"! Let's get started with our CHOCOLATE GLAZED/ORANGE FILLED COOKIES...

11	*Prepared Matza*
3/4	*Cup Orange Juice PLUS 1 Teaspoon Vanilla Extract*
3/4	*Cup Sugar*
6	*Tablespoons Margarine Or Butter, Softened (*Light)*

Generously grease and sugar two large cookie sheets and set aside. Combine orange juice and vanilla in a small spray bottle. Take prepared matza and spray generously both sides with orange juice/vanilla mixture. For better saturation, set matza aside for 1/2 hour. Using a pastry brush or butter knife, generously spread both sides of matza with margarine and sprinkle both sides generously with sugar. Now, take one piece of prepared matza and with a round cookie cutter, approximately three inches in diameter, cut four circles per matza and place matza circles on cookie sheets. Repeat this process for all remaining matza. Bake for 15 minutes or until golden brown. DO NOT OVER BAKE, MATZA ROUNDS WILL TASTE BITTER. While matza cookies are baking, let's prepare the FILLING...

8	*Tblsp Margarine Or Butter, Softened (*4 Tblsp Light)*
2	*Cups Powdered Sugar*
1/2	*Teaspoon Grated Orange Peel*
2 - 4	*Tablespoons Orange Juice/Vanilla Extract Mixture*

In a mixing bowl, combine butter and powdered sugar; cream until light and fluffy. Now, add orange peel, orange juice and cream once more until light and fluffy. When matza cookies are done baking, cool completely. Take cooled matza cookie and spread orange filling over matza rounds. Repeat this process using half of the matza rounds. Cover filled cookies with other half of matza rounds and place on wire rack that has been coated with margarine. Now, you will prepare e the CHOCOLATE GLAZE for drizzling your cookies...

2	*Ounces Un-Sweetened Chocolate*
3	*Tablespoons Margarine Or Butter (*Light)*
1	*Cup Powdered Sugar*
3/4	*Teaspoon Vanilla Plus 2 Tablespoons Hot Water*

In a small sauce pan, heat chocolate and butter over low heat until melted; remove from heat. Stir in powdered sugar and vanilla. Beat in hot water one teaspoon at a time until smooth; add enough hot water to mixture to make thin enough to drizzle over tops of cookies; let set...ENJOY!

Matza Cherry Jubilee Cookies

Preheat Oven 400 Degrees - Preparation Time 30 Minutes - Yield 24

Candied cherries, we feel, can be the prettiest decoration or garnish; especially when you use them as a topping for our matza cookies. The combination of the melted vanilla and chocolate drizzled on top of a candied cherry makes the cookie just "glisten" enough to want to grab it and eat it!! Enough with being a "Yenta" and let's move on by baking of our WAFER...

6	*Prepared Matza*
4	*Tablespoons Margarine Or Butter, Softened (*Light)*
1/2	*Cup Orange Juice*
1/2	*Teaspoon Vanilla Extract Plus 1/2 Cup Sugar*

Generously grease two large cookie sheets and generously sprinkle some of the sugar onto the cookie sheets. Combine orange juice and vanilla in a small spray bottle. Take prepared matza and spray both sides with orange juice/vanilla mixture. For better saturation, set matza aside for 1/2 hour. Using a pastry brush or butter knife, spread both sides of matza with margarine then sprinkle both sides with sugar. Now, take one piece of prepared matza and with a round cookie cutter, approximately three inches in diameter, cut four circles per matza, yielding 24 circles. Place circles onto cookie sheets and bake for 15 minutes or until golden brown. DO NOT OVER BAKE, MATZA ROUNDS WILL TASTE BITTER. While matza cookies are baking, let's prepare the TOPPING...

1/2	*Cup Vanilla Milk Chips*
1/2	*Cup Sweetened Condensed Milk*
1	*Tablespoon Butter Or Margarine (*Light)*
1/2	*Cup Candied Cherries, Chopped (Well Drained)*

In a small sauce pan, heat vanilla chips, milk and margarine or butter over low heat, stirring constantly, until chips are melted and mixture is smooth; remove from heat. Stir in cherries. When Matza cookies are finished baking, cool completely. After cookies have cooled, place on wire rack that has been coated with margarine. Spoon about one teaspoon of vanilla/cherry mixture onto cookie. Repeat this process for all remaining matza rounds, making sure that you have spread bits of cherry/vanilla mixture evenly over matza rounds. Now for the CHOCOLATE GLAZE...

2	*Ounces Of Un-Sweetened Chocolate*
3	*Tablespoons Margarine Or Butter (*Light)*
1	*Cup Powdered Sugar*
3/4	*Teaspoon Vanilla Plus 2 Tablespoons Hot Water*

In a small sized sauce pan, heat chocolate and butter or margarine over low heat until melted; remove from heat. Stir in powdered sugar and vanilla. Beat in hot water, one teaspoon at a time, until smooth. Add enough hot water to make chocolate mixture thin enough to drizzle over cookie; let topping set for about 20 to 30 minutes before serving...ENJOY!

Matza Date Mousse Puffs

Preheat Oven 450 Degrees - Preparation Time 20 Minutes - Yield 12

We have come up with a couple of mousse recipes and feel that they are exceptional, especially our Date Mousse Puffs. These Puffs are a combination of dates, toasted walnuts and cream cheese. This fluffy, sweet date mousse is a great "pop-in-the-oven" recipe. Let's gather the following ingredients for DATE MOUSSE PUFFS...

3	*Dry Matza (Broken Into Fourths By Using Your Hands)*
3	*Tablespoons Margarine, Softened (*Light)*
1/2	*Cup Sugar*
1/2	*Teaspoon Cinnamon*
1	*Cup Cream Cheese, Softened (*Light)*
1	*Tablespoon Powdered Sugar*
1	*Cup Dates, Coarsely Chopped*
3/4	*Toasted Walnuts, Chopped*

Grease a 9 x 13 cookie sheet with margarine; set aside. Combine your cinnamon and sugar in a small bowl; sprinkle some of the cinnamon/sugar mix onto cookie sheet. Take your dry matza and break into fourths, coat both sides with softened margarine and sprinkle both sides with cinnamon/ sugar mix; set aside.

Place cream cheese and powdered sugar in food processor and process until well mixed and creamy. Remove cream cheese mixture from food processor and place in mixing bowl; fold in chopped dates and spread on to greased and sugared matza quarters.

Top Date Mousse Puffs with lightly toasted, chopped walnuts and bake in preheated oven for 15 minutes...ENJOY

Matza Florentines

You say Matza Florentines? Impossible! And we say, Yes, Matza Florentines!!!. A delicious crispy wafer, dipped in semi-sweet chocolate, then topped with toasted, crushed almonds--and all made out of matza. Wow! Such a Cookie, Such a Deal! Well, enough yaking, let's get started with our "POSSIBLE MATZA FLORENTINES"...

10	*Prepared Matza*
3/4	*Cup Orange Juice*
1	*Teaspoon Vanilla Extract*
3/4	*Cup Sugar*
6	*Tablespoons Margarine Or Butter, Softened (*Light)*

Generously grease two large cookie sheets and generously sprinkle with some of the sugar, set aside. Combine orange juice and vanilla in a small spray bottle. Take prepared matza and spray both sides with orange juice/vanilla mixture. For better saturation, set matza aside for 1/2 hour. Using a pastry brush or butter knife, generously brush or spread margarine or butter on both sides of matza and sprinkle both sides generously with sugar. Now, take one piece of prepared matza and with a round cookie cutter, approximately three inches in diameter, cut four circles per matza and place circles onto buttered and sugared cookie sheets. Repeat this process for remaining matza. Bake Florentines for 15 minutes or until golden brown. ***DO NOT OVER BAKE, MATZA ROUNDS WILL TASTE BITTER.*** While Matza Florentines are baking, we'll prepare the chocolate topping...

1 1/2	*Cups Semi-Sweet Dark Chocolate Chips Or 12 Ounces Of Dark Semi-Sweet Chocolate (1/2 Ounce Cubes) Melted In Microwave Or Using Double-Boiler Method*
1/2	*Cup Toasted, Crushed Almonds*

When Matza Florentines are finished baking, cool completely before removing from cookie sheets. Take cooled Matza Florentine and with a pastry brush or butter knife, spread or brush chocolate on one half of the Matza Florentine, sprinkle with toasted, crushed almonds and place on a rack that has been buttered or greased, cool Florentine completely. We guarantee that you will gobble these Florentines up one right after the other...ENJOY!

NOTE: Prepared Matza may crack while cutting circles with cookie cutter. It's okay--"a little crack adds a little character". All kidding aside, once Florentines are baked, you won't be able to tell if there was a crack!

Matza Fondue Strips

Preheat Oven 400 Degrees/Stove Top - Preparation Time 30 Minutes - Yield 80 Strips

Read on and don't let the title fool you, because you don't need a Fondue pot to enjoy this different way of serving these sweetened matza strips accompanied by a smooth chocolate sauce.   Entertain your friends with this Passover dessert and your sure to be a hit. Gather the following ingredients for MATZA FONDUE STRIPS..

8	*Prepared Matza*
1/2	*Cup Orange Juice*
1	*Teaspoon Vanilla Extract*
1/2	*Cup Sugar, For Coating Pan And Sprinkling Matza*
4	*Tablespoons Margarine, Softened (*Light)*

GREASE two 9 x 13 cookie sheets and sprinkle with sugar. Combine orange juice and vanilla in small spray bottle. Take prepared matza and spray both sides with orange juice/vanilla mixture. *For better saturation, set matza aside for about 1/2 an hour.*   Now, brush both sides of matza with margarine using a pastry brush or butter knife and sprinkle both sides with sugar. For the cutting process, you will first cut matza in half vertically, then into 1/2 inch strips, five across horizontally, yielding 10 strips per matza. Place strips onto cookie sheets, **BE SURE NOT TO OVERLAP**, and bake in preheated oven for about 15 to 20 minutes or until golden brown. Provided strips are baked until golden brown, they will automatically harden as they cool. Matza strips store well, and when you are ready to prepare the CHOCOLATE SAUCE, gather the following ingredients...

4	*Ounces Un-Sweetened Chocolate*
1	*Cup Sweetened Condensed Milk*
1	*Cup Half And Half Or Light Cream*
2	*Teaspoons Vanilla*
	Powdered Sugar, For Sifting Over Strips

Combine chocolate, sweetened condensed milk, cream, and vanilla in a double boiler or fondue pot, stirring constantly over low heat until chocolate mixture has thickened. If you do not have a double boiler, you can place ingredients in a smaller sized sauce pan and place the smaller sized sauce pan into a larger sized sauce pan filled half way with water. The purpose of double boiling is to insure that the chocolate mixture will not burn. Place matza strips in a bowl and sift with powdered sugar. To serve, dip matza strips in hot chocolate sauce, OR serve by drizzling strips with chocolate sauce...ENJOY!

Matza Haroseth Cookie Rolls

Preheat Oven 375 Degrees - Preparation Time 30 Minutes - Yield 48

Many of us find ourselves with leftover Haroseth after the first Seder night.   We love our own traditional Haroseth and find ourselves picking at it the following day, or simply spreading it on a dry matza.   Try this fantastic, fun way of putting your favorite Haroseth recipe and turn it into a simply delicious rolled cookie with the same flavor.   For this you can use your favorite Haroseth recipe and simply add cream cheese filling.   For a not so boring way of putting Haroseth leftovers together, let's gather the following ingredients for HAROSETH COOKIE ROLLS that the entire family will enjoy...

For Matza Cutting see Diagram 14

12	*Prepared Matza*
8	*Tablespoons Margarine, Softened (*Light)*
1/2	*Cup Sugar*
3/4	*Cups Orange Juice*
1	*Tablespoon Vanilla Extract*

Combine orange juice and vanilla in small spray bottle. Take prepared matza and spray both sides with orange juice/vanilla mixture. Set aside to allow saturation, about 1/2 hour. Trim as close to the edge all four sides of matza (for a nice finished edge), then cut each matza into fourths. Gently brush both sides of matza with softened margarine using either a butter knife or pastry brush and set aside. We leave it up to you to use your favorite Haroseth and add the following ingredients in preparing the FILLING...

2	*Cups Haroseth*
1	*Cup Cream Cheese, Softened (*Light)*
3	*Tablespoons Powdered Sugar*
1	*Tablespoon Granulated Sugar*
1/2	*Teaspoon Cinnamon (Optional)*
1/4	*Cup Sesame Seeds (If Available For Passover)*

Grease two 13 x 9 cookie sheets. In medium sized mixing bowl, combine Haroseth, cream cheese and 2 tablespoons powdered sugar.   Combine granulated sugar and cinnamon and sprinkle both sides of flavored matza.   Take one fourth of matza at a time and place in front of you diagonally, as if you are looking at a diamond shape. Place one tablespoon filling at one corner of the matza and roll away from you as if you are rolling a crescent roll (diagonally), then place on greased cookie sheet seam side down. Continue this process until you run out of filling. Top with sprinkled sesame seeds and bake in preheated oven for about an hour and 15 minutes, or until evenly browned. Cookie rolls will harden as they cool. Once cooled, sprinkle with remaining powdered sugar and ENJOY a flavor most resembling Rugelach...ENJOY!

Matza Honey Chewies

Stove Top - Preparation Time 20 Minutes - Yield 18

One of our favorite easy to prepare candy recipes. This has a nice nutty honey flavor geared for those who may want to try something other than a chocolate type of candy. A candy thermometer would be beneficial to measure accurate heat level. If you don't have a candy thermometer handy, you can use the boiling point for a measure of heat as your guide. You will need the following ingredients for a very different type of candy, HONEY CHEWIES...

4	*Cups Dry Matza, Bite Size Pieces*
1 1/2	*Cups Salted Nuts*
1 1/2	*Cups Brown Sugar*
3/4	*Cups Honey*
1/2	*Cup Water*
4	*Teaspoons Fresh Lemon Juice*

Grease a large sized mixing bowl with butter or margarine. Combine matza pieces and salted peanuts in buttered mixing bowl, set aside. In a large sauce pan, mix together the brown sugar, honey, water, and lemon juice. Cook this mixture over medium heat, stirring occasionally. Place thermometer in mixture. Continue cooking until you reach 250 degrees (firm ball stage) stirring constantly. If you are not using a thermometer, when the mixture reaches boiling point, keep over heat for about 5 minutes stirring mixture constantly. Pour syrup over matza/nut mixture and mix with well greased wooden spoon or wet spoon to avoid sticking. Cool slightly to thicken.

Pour all the ingredients that you now have in your bowl into a 13 x 9 greased cookie sheet. Pat this mixture gently with a buttered or wet spoon so that mixture won't stick to spoon. Spread evenly throughout the pan and let cool for about 30 minutes. You can pre-mark squares, about 2 ", when mixture has cooled for about 15 minutes. After about 45 minutes, cut or chip marked squares...ENJOY!

NOTE: To check proper heat level, you can drop a little bit of hot mixture into a separate bowl of cold water, and if the mixture forms into a hard ball, then you ' GOT CANDY!!!

Matza Honey Nut Strudel

Preheat Oven 400 Degrees - Preparation Time 30 Minutes - Yield 20

Enjoy the taste of honey with a buttery - toasty - nutty flavor. We are sure you'll love this crispy strudel made with matza. Our HONEY NUT STRUDEL can be put together in a matter of minutes and enjoyed for breakfast or any after dinner dessert, strictly your preference...

4	*Prepared Matza*
3	*Tablespoons Margarine, Softened (*Light)*
1/4	*Cup Orange Juice*
1/2	*Teaspoon Vanilla Extract*
1/4	*Cup Sugar*

Generously grease a cookie sheet with margarine; set aside. Combine orange juice and vanilla in a spray bottle. Take prepared matza and spray both sides with orange juice/vanilla mixture. You can set matza aside for better saturation, about 1/2 hour. Using a butter knife or pastry brush, generously coat both sides of matza with softened margarine and generously sprinkle both sides of matza with sugar and set aside. Now let's prepare the nut strudel FILLING...

1	*Cup Toasted Almonds Or Walnuts, Finely Chopped*
1	*Cup Honey*
1/4	*Cup Honey For Topping*
1/2	*Cup Toasted Nuts For Topping, Chopped*

Now, take one piece of prepared matza and place matza grain vertically in front of you. Spread 1/4 cup of honey over each matza, sprinkle 1/4 cup nuts over each matza and roll up away from you. Repeat this process until remaining matza are filled with honey and nuts. Place matza strudels on greased cookie sheet seam side down and bake in 400 degree oven for about 15 minutes or until crispy and golden brown. After baking, remove from oven and let cool for about 2 minutes. Glaze tops of strudels generously with honey, sprinkle with toasted nuts, REMOVE FROM COOKIE SHEET and place on cutting board to cut into slices...ENJOY!

NOTE: Don't panic! Honey will seep out of the ends of matza strudel while baking, that's okay--strudel is open on both ends, so that is bound to happen. Just remember to remove strudel from cookie sheet after it has set, about two minutes. Otherwise, when the honey has completely cooled it will harden and it will become difficult to remove the strudels from the cookie sheets.

Matza `Jammer` Cookies

Preheat Oven 400 Degrees - Preparation Time 30 Minutes - Yield 18

This cookie is simply your basic Matza Florentine stuffed with your favorite kind of jam and glazed with a delicious melt-in-your-mouth vanilla glaze. They're a bit smaller than your Matza Florentine but just as enticing!! You'll want to "gobble" them up--one right after the other!! The following ingredients are needed for our JAMMER COOKIES...

6	*Prepared Matza*
4	*Tablespoons Margarine Or Butter, Softened (*Light)*
1/2	*Cup Orange Juice*
1/2	*Teaspoon Vanilla Extract*
1/2	*Cup Sugar*

Generously grease two large cookie sheets with margarine and generously sprinkle some of the sugar onto the cookie sheets. Combine orange juice and vanilla in a small spray bottle and spray both sides with orange juice/vanilla mixture. For better saturation, set matza aside for 1/2 hour. Using a pastry brush or butter knife, coat both sides of matza generously with margarine and sprinkle both sides generously with sugar. Now, take one piece of prepared matza and with a round cookie cutter, about three inches in diameter, cut four circles per matza, then cut two to three more circles out of the same piece of matza but only using a smaller cookie cutter, about two inches in diameter, yielding about six to seven circles per matza. Place matza circles onto greased and sugared cookie sheets. Repeat this process for all remaining matza. Bake in preheated oven for 15 minutes or until golden brown. ***DO NOT OVER BAKE, MATZA ROUNDS WILL BE BITTER.*** While matza rounds are baking, let's prepare our jam for the FILLING...

1/2	*Cup Of Raspberry Or Apricot (*Light)*
2	*Tablespoons Water*
18	*Sliced Toasted Almonds*

In a small sauce pan, combine jam and water and melt down over low heat. After matza rounds have completely cooled, place larger matza round onto rack that has been buttered to prevent sticking of cookie. Now, place one slice of toasted almond on the bottom of the center of each cookie on rack and then spoon approximately one teaspoon of jam on top of that sliced almond. Now cover the jam with the smaller matza round. Let's prepare the VANILLA GLAZE...

1/2	*Cup Powdered Sugar*
1/4	*Teaspoon Vanilla*
3	*Teaspoons Real Cream (*Light)*

In a small mixing bowl combine above ingredients and mix until creamy and smooth. Take a spoon and drizzle vanilla glaze over Matza Jammers. Let vanilla glaze harden, about 10 to 15 minutes...ENJOY!

Matza Mock Maple `N` Nut Crunch

Preheat Oven 400 Degrees - Preparation Time 30 Minutes - 24

Our Mock Maple Syrup and nut topping is just the added touch to making this cookie unique in its flavor. With coffee, tea, or milk, it will definitely satisfy your craving for something crunchy yet sweet. So, give it a try and gather the following ingredients for our MOCK MAPLE N' NUT CRUNCH COOKIE...

6	*Prepared Matza*
4	*Tablespoons Margarine, Softened (*Light)*
1/2	*Cup Orange Juice*
1/2	*Teaspoon Vanilla Extract*
1/2	*Cup Sugar*

Generously grease two large cookie sheets and sprinkle some of the sugar onto the cookie sheets. Combine orange juice and vanilla in a small spray bottle. Take prepared matza and spray both sides with orange juice/vanilla mixture. For better saturation, set matza aside for 1/2 hour. Using a pastry brush or butter knife, generously spread both sides of matza with butter or margarine and sprinkle both sides generously with sugar. Now, take one piece of prepared matza and with a round cookie cutter, approximately three inches in diameter, cut four circles per matza and place on greased/sugared cookie sheet. Repeat this process for all 24 circles. Bake in preheated oven for 15 minutes or until golden brown. Cool completely before removing from cookie sheets. After cookies are completely cooled, place on buttered rack .
Let's prepare the TOPPING...

1	*Cup Brown Sugar, Packed*
4	*Tablespoons Water*
2	*Tablespoons Butter Or Margarine (*Light)*
1/2 Cup To 3/4 Cup Coarsely Ground Toasted Almonds	

In a small sauce pan cook brown sugar and water over low heat until smooth, bring to a simmering boil and boil for two to three minutes. Remove from heat and stir in butter and nuts. Spoon and drizzle this mixture over entire cookie. Cool cookie completely on buttered rack before removing...ENJOY!

Matza Napoleon

Preheat Oven 400 Degrees - Preparation Time 45 Minutes - Yield 18

This is a real "I can't believe it's a Matza dessert!". This scrumptious dessert tastes best if prepared 24 hours in advance. Matza Napoleons have that gourmet appearance but are very light, and easy to prepare. You will need the following ingredients to prepare the NAPOLEON strips...

For Matza Cutting see Diagram 12	

6   **Prepared Matza**

4   **Tablespoons Margarine, Softened (*Light)**

1/2   **Cup Orange Juice**

1/2   **Teaspoon Vanilla Extract**

1/2   **Cup Sugar**

Generously grease 13 x 9 cookie sheet; generously sprinkle with sugar. Combine orange juice and vanilla in a small spray bottle. Take prepared matza and spray both sides with orange juice/vanilla mixture; set aside for 1/2 hour for better saturation. Using a pastry brush or butter knife, spread both sides of matza with margarine, then sprinkle both sides with sugar. Trim the ends of the prepared matza making sure to cut as close to the edges as possible. Cut matza horizontally into fourths by following the grain. Now cut matza in half vertically, yielding 8 equal pieces per matza.

Place rectangular pieces of matza onto cookie sheet; do not overlap. Bake for 12-15 minutes or until golden brown and allow pieces to completely cool; matza strips will harden as they cool. Lets prepare VANILLA CREME filling...

3.4   **Ounce French Vanilla Instant Pudding**

1   **Cup Milk (*Lowfat)**

2   **Pints Real Whipping Cream (1 Pint For Topping) (*Light)**

4   **Tablespoons Powdered Sugar (2 Tablespoon For Topping)**

1   **Cup Almonds, Sliced And Toasted**

Prepare the Instant Pudding according to directions on package. **EXCEPT USE ONLY 1 CUP OF MILK**. Whip 1 pint of real whipping cream, adding 2 tablespoons of powdered sugar until light and fluffy. Add whipped cream mixture to the pudding mixture and whip until light, fluffy and well mixed.

To assemble: Each Napoleon consists of 3 strips of matza and 3 layers of cream filling. For the topping you will whip 1 pint of real whipping cream, adding 2 tablespoons of powdered sugar. Use a pastry bag with desired tip to decorate the top layer of your Napoleon strip and garnish tops and sides to perfection with toasted sliced almonds...ENJOY!

Matza Newtons

Matza Newtons? Pretty "catchy"! Yes, it is a Fig Newton but with a date filling with just a zip of cinnamon and ginger. This is a great recipe to get the whole family involved in. We call it "assembly line baking", everything gets done in a matter of minutes with everyone helping. So, let's get started with our MATZA NEWTONS...

10	*Prepared Matza*
3/4	*Cup Orange Juice*
1	*Teaspoon Vanilla Extract*
3/4	*Cup Sugar*
1	*Teaspoon Cinnamon*
6	*Tablespoons Margarine Or Butter, Softened (*Light)*

For Matza Cutting see Diagram 11

Generously grease two large cookie sheets with margarine or butter. Combine sugar and cinnamon in a small bowl. Sprinkle some of the cinnamon and sugar onto cookie sheets and set aside. Combine orange juice and vanilla in a small spray bottle. Take prepared matza and spray both sides with orange juice/vanilla mixture. For better saturation, set matza aside for 1/2 hour. Using a pastry brush or butter knife, brush or spread both sides of matza with margarine or butter and sprinkle both sides with cinnamon and sugar mix; set aside. Let's prepare the DATE FILLING...

1	*Cup Whole Pitted Dates*
1	*Cup Raisins*
2	*Tablespoons Sugar*
2	*Tablespoons Margarine Or Butter (*Light)*
1/2	*Teaspoon Ground Ginger*
1/2	*Teaspoon Cinnamon*
1/4	*Cup Sugar Plus 1/2 Teaspoon Cinnamon For Sprinkling Tops Of Cookies*

Place dates, raisins, sugar, margarine, ginger, and cinnamon in food processor. Process until smooth, set aside. Take one piece of matza with matza grain vertically in front of you and with a round cookie cutter, approximately three inches in diameter, cut four circles per matza. Repeat this cutting process for all remaining matza. Take matza circles, again with grain vertically in front of you and place about one teaspoon of date filling in center, fold circle in half, press to seal and place on cinnamon/sugared cookie sheet. Repeat this process until you have filled all your matza circles. Once Matza Newtons are placed onto cookie sheet, sprinkle tops of Matza Newtons with cinnamon and sugar mix. Bake cookies for twenty minutes or until golden brown...ENJOY!

Matza Pecan Brown Sugar Crunchies

Preheat Oven 400 Degrees - Preparation Time 30 Minutes - Yield 24

Yes, another matza cookie, and you will probably get a few more cookie recipes before we're through. It's just another delicious way of preparing matza! Matza cookies are easy to make and they taste good, too--especially our PECAN BROWN SUGAR CRUNCHIES! Come on, let's get started, so you can enjoy eating them too!...

6	*Prepared Matza*
4	*Tablespoons Margarine Or Butter, Softened (*Light)*
1/2	*Cup Orange Juice*
1/2	*Teaspoon Vanilla Extract*
1/2	*Cup Sugar*

Generously grease and sprinkle some sugar on two large cookie sheets. Combine orange juice and vanilla in a small spray bottle. Take prepared matza and spray both sides with orange juice/vanilla mixture. For better saturation, set matza aside for 1/2 hour. Using a pastry brush or butter knife, generously spread both sides of matza with margarine and generously sprinkle both sides with sugar. Now, take one piece of prepared matza and with a round cookie cutter, approximately three inches in diameter, cut four circles per matza, yielding 24 circles; set aside. Let's prepare PECAN TOPPING...

1	*Cup Crushed Pecans*
1	*Cup Light Brown Sugar, Packed*

In a small mixing bowl, combine pecans and brown sugar. Take approximately 1/2 teaspoonful of this mixture and place it onto cookie sheets in separate piles; making twelve separate piles per cookie sheet. Place piles as if you were placing a cookie there. You are then going to place a matza round on each of the brown sugar/pecan piles, pressing matza rounds gently and turning slightly into brown sugar and pecan mixture. This will give the bottom of the matza cookie a crunchie consistency and flavor. Now, take another heaping 1/2 teaspoonful of the brown sugar/pecan mix and place on top of each of the matza rounds. Making a round pile nicely packed into the center of each matza cookie. Place cookies in preheated oven for 15 minutes or until tops are lightly browned, cool completely...ENJOY!

Matza Pineapple Strudel

Preheat Oven 400 Degrees - Preparation Time 30 Minutes - Yield 10

This dessert is a Do-Ahead recipe in which you will need to drain the cottage cheese to prepare for the filling. It is suggested that you place the cottage cheese in cheese cloth and let drain overnight. Who would think that pineapple and cottage cheese can bake to perfection with matza? Well, guess what... again we topped ourselves, and we're proud of it, so imagine what your family will say when you prepare PINEAPPLE STRUDEL...

For Matza Cutting see Diagram 10	4	*Prepared Matza*
	2	*Tablespoons Margarine, Softened (*Light)*
	1/4	*Cup Orange Juice*
	1/2	*Teaspoon Vanilla Extract*
	1/4	*Cup Sugar*

Lightly grease a non-stick cookie sheet with margarine and set aside. Combine orange juice and vanilla in a spray bottle. Take prepared matza and spray both sides with orange juice/vanilla mixture. You can set matza aside for better saturation, about 1/2 hour. Using a butter knife or pastry brush, coat both sides of matza with softened margarine and generously sprinkle both sides of matza with sugar and set aside. Now we will prepare the pineapple strudel FILLING...

1/3	*Cup Sugar*
1	*Tablespoon Matza Meal*
1	*Cup Drained Cottage Cheese (*Lowfat)*
1	*Cup Canned Pineapple, Drained,Finely Chopped (*In Its Own Juice)*
4	*Tablespoon Sugar, For Topping*
2	*Teaspoon Cinnamon, For Topping*
2	*Tblsp Melted Butter/Margarine For Topping (*Light)*

In medium sized mixing bowl, combine sugar, matza meal, cottage cheese, pineapple, mix well and set aside. Take two pieces of prepared matza and place matza so that the grain is vertically in front of you, end to end, with 1/2" overlap in the middle, to form one long piece of matza.

Evenly Spread half of the pineapple/cheese mixture onto overlapped matzas, and roll up away from you. Repeat this process for the remaining strudel. Place strudels onto greased cookie sheet. Combine two tablespoons sugar and one teaspoon cinnamon in a small bowl and sprinkle tops of each strudel. Place in preheated oven for 30 minutes or until golden. After baking, let strudels cool for 10 minutes. For garnishing tops of strudels, drizzle two tablespoons melted margarine or butter and sprinkle with remaining two tablespoons sugar and one teaspoon cinnamon. Cool completely before slicing into 1" strips...ENJOY!

Matza Sesame Teasers

Preheat Oven 350 Degrees - Preparation Time 15 Minutes - Yield 16

Personally we love sesame anything... This recipe is OH SO EASY. We like to re-heat these up in the morning and have with either coffee or tea. Prepare as much as you'd like and store in an airtight container. When you are ready to bite into SESAME TEASERS, simply heat up your toaster oven and pop these in for about 5 minutes. Gather the following ingredients...

4	Dry Matza
6	Tablespoon Margarine, Softened (*Light)
1/2	Cup Sugar
1/2	Teaspoon Cinnamon
1/2	Cup Sesame Seeds, Toasted (If Available For Passover)
1/3	Cup Honey
1/2	Cup Almonds, Toasted And Crushed

Wrap your broiler pan with aluminum foil and set aside. Combine cinnamon and sugar in a small bowl. Using 2 tablespoons margarine, generously coat your four pieces of matza on one side then top the same side by sprinkling with cinnamon/ sugar mixture.

In a small sauce pan, melt the rest of your butter or margarine; remove from heat. Using the same sauce pan, add toasted sesame seeds, honey and almonds; mix thoroughly.

Now, place your coated matza "sugared side down" on broiler pan. Take your sesame seed mixture and spread on the "plain side or up side" of matza, making sure to cover entire matza with mixture. Be sure to work as quickly as possible because the mixture will become to hard to spread.

Bake in broiler for approximately one to three minutes. *CAUTION:* You must keep a close watch with this recipe because it will burn quickly. Our suggestion would be to check on the Sesame Teasers every thirty seconds or so...ENJOY!

Matza Old Fashioned Taiglach

Preheat Oven 400 Degrees - Preparation Time 30 Minutes - Yield 48

Taiglach meaning "little pieces of dough" in Yiddish--are pastries coated with honey and combined with nuts and raisins, cooked in a delicious syrup. Well, we have created a Taiglach made with matza just to serve on our Passover Holiday. Incredible! Let's get started by gathering the following ingredients for MATZA TAIGLACH

6	*Prepared Matza*
4	*Tablespoons Margarine Or Butter, Softened (*Light)*
1/2	*Cup Sugar*
1/2	*Cup Orange Juice*
1/2	*Teaspoon Vanilla Extract*

Generously grease two large cookie sheets and sprinkle some of the sugar onto the cookie sheets. Combine orange juice and vanilla in a small spray bottle. Take prepared matza and spray both sides with orange juice/vanilla mixture. For better saturation, set matza aside for 1/2 hour. Using a pastry brush or butter knife, spread or brush both sides of matza with butter or margarine and sprinkle both sides with sugar. Place whole pieces of matza onto buttered and sugared cookie sheets. Approximately three matza per cookie sheet, but you will have to cut some matza in half to fit proportionately onto cookie sheet. Bake in preheated oven for 15 minutes or until lightly browned (matza will be Al-dente, soft but yet hard). Remove cookie sheet from oven and set aside. Now, we will prepare the SYRUP...

1	*Cup Honey*
1 1/2	*Cups Sugar*
2	*Teaspoons Ground Ginger*
1/4	*Teaspoon Cinnamon*
1 1/2	*Cups Whole Toasted Almonds*
1	*Cup Shredded Toasted Coconut*

Butter or margarine a wooden board, in order to place hot Matza Taiglach; set aside. In a large, non stick skillet (12" x 4") cook honey, sugar, ginger and cinnamon over medium/low heat until smooth and sugar has melted. While this mixture is cooking, about five minutes, we will cut the matza into one inch strips and then cut the one inch strips into thirds and set aside. Now, bring sugar/honey mixture to a simmer, then add the almonds, coconut and cut matza. Stir and continue to cook until all pieces of matza have been well coated with honey /syrup mixture (mixture will be stiff). Remove Matza Taiglach from heat and with a wooden spoon drop heaping moundfuls, approximately 24 mounds, three inches in diameter, onto buttered board. You must work quickly as syrup will harden when it starts cooling. Cool Matza Taiglach over night. With a sharp knife, cut mounds into fourths...ENJOY!

Matza Vanilla Crisps

Preheat Oven 400 Degrees - Preparation Time 20 Minutes - Yield 24

These crisp vanilla wafers are my husband, Bruyn's, favorite cookie with his morning cup of coffee. He seems to gobble them up before we even place them on a platter. They are a crisp, lightly sweetened wafer that are sweet enough to satisfy those urges and light enough to accompany any meal. Let's prepare VANILLA CRISPS by gathering the following ingredients...

6	*Prepared Matza*
1/2	*Cup Sugar*
1/2	*Cube Butter Or Margarine, Softened (*Light)*
1/2	*Cup Orange Juice*
1/2	*Teaspoon Vanilla Extract*

Generously grease two large cookie sheets with margarine or butter; sprinkle some of the sugar onto cookie sheets and set aside. Combine orange juice and vanilla in a small spray bottle. Take prepared matza and spray both sides with orange juice/vanilla mixture. For better saturation, set matza aside for 1/2 hour.

Using a pastry brush or butter knife, generously spread or brush both sides of matza with butter or margarine and generously sprinkle both sides with sugar. Take one piece of prepared matza and with a round cookie cutter, approximately three inches in diameter, cut four circles per matza and place circles onto buttered and sugared cookie sheets. Repeat this process for all remaining matza.

Bake vanilla crisps in preheated oven for 15 minutes or until golden brown. ***DO NOT OVER BAKE, MATZA COOKIES WILL TASTE BITTER.*** After baking, remove from oven and let cool completely before removing from cookie sheets...ENJOY!

Matza Ice Cream Sandwiches

Preheat Oven 400 Degrees - Preparation Time 30 Minutes - Yield 12

Shana Zeesa--This recipe is for you!!! Ice Cream Sandwiches? Unheard of on Passover! Not with our recipe. Preparation of this Ice Cream Sandwich is real simple too. Without any further description, let's jump right into this yummy dessert--our MATZA ICE CREAM SANDWICHES...

6	*Prepared Matza*
4	*Tablespoons Butter Or Margarine, Softened (*Light)*
1/2	*Cup Orange Juice*
1/2	*Teaspoon Vanilla Extract*
1/2	*Cup Sugar*

Generously grease two large cookie sheets with margarine or butter; sprinkle some of the sugar onto the cookie sheets. Combine orange juice and vanilla in a small spray bottle. Take prepared matza and spray both sides with orange juice/vanilla mixture. For better saturation, set matza aside for 1/2 hour. Using a pastry brush or butter knife, generously spread or brush both sides of matza with margarine and sprinkle both sides generously with sugar. Take one piece of matza and with a round cookie cutter, approximately three inches in diameter, cut four circles per matza. Place circles onto cookie sheets and repeat this process until you have 24 matza rounds. Bake in preheated oven for 15 minutes or until nicely browned. Cool completely before removing from cookie sheet. When completely cooled, place on buttered rack. Let's prepare the TOPPING...

1	*Cup Packed Brown Sugar*
4	*Tablespoons Water*
2	*Tablespoons Butter Or Margarine (*Light)*
1/2-3/4	*Cup Coarsely Ground Toasted Almonds*

In a small sauce pan, cook brown sugar and water over low heat until smooth, bring to a simmering boil, and boil for two to three minutes. Remove from heat, stir in butter and nuts and drizzle this mixture over entire cookie. Cool completely, preferably overnight to get that real crunchy cookie or cool three to four hours making sure that when you touch cookie they are not sticky and ground almonds do not come off. Now for the VANILLA FILLING...

1	*Quart Vanilla Ice Cream (Firm But A Little Soft)(*Fatfree)*
1 1/2	*Cups Mini Dark Chocolate Chips (*Reduced Fat)*

Each Ice Cream Sandwich contains about 1/4 to 1/2 cup of ice cream. We like vanilla ice cream, so we made them with a full 1/2 cup. Place vanilla ice cream on one matza cookie, then cover with another matza cookie, pressing together to make the shape of a round ice cream sandwich with some of the ice cream coming out of the sides of the sandwich. Now, take your mini chocolate chips and place them in a bowl and take your Matza Ice Cream Sandwich and press exposed sides of ice cream into chocolate chips. Place finished sandwiches onto buttered dish and place in freezer for several hours until sufficiently frozen...ENJOY!

Matza Walnut Bon Bons

Oven/Stove Top - Prep Time 20 Minutes - Yield 30

These glazed candies have a scrumptious, walnutty flavor with a taste of chocolate that covers both matza and walnuts. If you like walnuts and chocolate with a hint of toasted coconut, you'll love this recipe! Do not preheat the oven for this one. This yummy project is a great recipe to get the whole family involved in, so let's get started by gathering the following ingredients for WALNUT BON BONS...

4	*Squares Un-Sweetened Chocolate (4 Oz)*
1 1/2	*Cups Sweetened Condensed Milk*
1	*Cup Walnuts, Whole Or Pieces*
2	*Cups Dry Matza, Crumbled Using Hands*
1	*Cup Toasted Coconut, Shredded*

In a double boiler, melt chocolate squares over hot water. If you do not have a double boiler, you can place the chocolate squares in a smaller sized sauce pan and place the smaller sized sauce pan into a larger sized sauce pan filled half way with water. The purpose of double boiling is to insure that the chocolate will not burn. Bring water to a boil and continue to simmer until all chocolate has melted. Another option of melting chocolate is to use your microwave. Once the chocolate has melted, take it off heat and stir in the condensed milk, walnuts, matza, and toasted coconut until well mixed.

With wet hands or wet tablespoon, drop teaspoonfuls of mixture onto a greased 13 x 9 cookie sheet. If you want it to look like a BON BON, then you will need to shape it like a BON BON with either your hands or tablespoon. Remember, this is a very rich candy and you don't want to shape these to big.

Place candy in cold oven and turn temperature up to 350 degrees. Leave the candy in the oven for about 3 to 5 minutes. Be sure to carefully keep watch because as soon as you see the candy glaze you will need to immediately remove from the oven, otherwise you will get a flattened candy instead of the BON BON appearance...ENJOY!

Matza N.Y. Cheese Cake

Preheat Oven 350 Degrees - Preparation Time 30 Minutes - Yield 16

This is a "24- hour DO AHEAD" type of recipe. You will need to let your cake cool overnight to gain its rich, smooth, cheese cake consistency. Leiat and Prospers favorite! For the CRUST, gather...

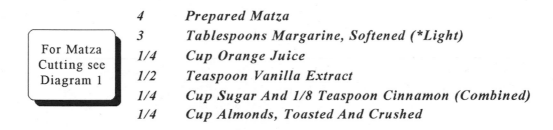

For Matza Cutting see Diagram 1

4	*Prepared Matza*
3	*Tablespoons Margarine, Softened (*Light)*
1/4	*Cup Orange Juice*
1/2	*Teaspoon Vanilla Extract*
1/4	*Cup Sugar And 1/8 Teaspoon Cinnamon (Combined)*
1/4	*Cup Almonds, Toasted And Crushed*

Grease sides and bottom of a 10" spring form pan with margarine and sprinkle with some of the cinamon/sugar mix; set aside. Combine orange juice and vanilla in small spray bottle. Spray both sides of prepared matza; set for about 1/2 hour. Using a butter knife, coat both sides of matza with margarine and sprinkle both sides with sugar mix. Place all four prepared matzas in front of you, so that they are arranged to form a square. Turn pan upside down over matza. Use a sharp knife and cut around pan, yielding wedges forming a circle. Turn pan right side up and place wedges with points inside the center to form a matza bottom. Sprinkle the bottom of the crust with both toasted almonds and sugar and set aside. Now, let's gather the following ingredients for the FILLING...

4	*Cups Softened Cream Cheese (8 Oz) (*Light)*
1 1/2	*Cups Sugar*
4	*Eggs, Beaten (*2 Whole Eggs And 2 Egg Whites)*
1	*Pint Sour Cream (*Light)*
2	*Teaspoons Vanilla*
2	*Teaspoons Lemon Peel, Grated*

With a mixer, combine softened cream cheese with the remaining ingredients and beat until smooth and creamy. Pour into the matza crust, and bake in preheated oven for about 50 to 60 minutes or until firm. Cool in refrigerator for at least 4-6 hours or preferably overnight. When cake has cooled, you will prepare the TOPPING, by first preheating oven to 375 degrees and mix with spoon...*We felt that this recipe is so worthwhile to make that it was worth the two pages taken...* ....

2	*Cups Sour Cream (*Light)*
2	*Teaspoons Vanilla AND 1 Tablespoon Sugar*

Cover the cold cake with sour cream mixture; bake for 35 minutes in preheated oven. Cool for 12 hours. Prepare vanilla CREME garnish by mixing the ingredients below; use a pastry bag with desired tip to decorate...

3.4	*Ounce Of French Vanilla Instant Pudding Mix (Small Box)*
3/4	*Cup Milk (*1% Fat)*
1/2	*Pint Real Whipping Cream (*Light)*
2	*Tablespoons Powdered Sugar*

Prepare the instant pudding according to directions on package **EXCEPT USE ONLY 3/4 CUP OF MILK**. Whip 1/2 pint of real whipping cream, adding 2 tablespoons of powdered sugar until fluffy. Add whipped cream mixture to the pudding mixture and whip together until light and fluffy and spread or use pastry bag garnish top of cheese cake. Top with thinly sliced strawberries...ENJOY!

Matza Apple Tart

Preheat Oven 400 Degrees/Stove Top - Prep Time 20 Minutes - Yield 8

A classic gourmet look and taste, yet OH SO Simple! Our Ema, "Solange" enjoys making this tart off season by using Pate Brisee as the crust, and has perfected a flavorful tart that you would get at any French bakery. We have perfected the crust, and using our flavored matza coupled with MOM's apple filling, you will appreciate presenting "OUR" APPLE TART during the Passover holidays...

For Matza Cutting see Diagram 1	4	*Prepared Matza*
	3	*Tablespoons Margarine, Softened (*Light)*
	1/4	*Cup Orange Juice*
	1/2	*Teaspoon Vanilla Extract*
	1/4	*Cup Sugar*

Lightly grease 9" tart pan or pie pan with a little margarine, lightly sprinkle with sugar and set aside. Combine orange juice and vanilla in small spray bottle. Take prepared matza and spray both sides with orange juice/vanilla mixture. You can set matza aside to allow better saturation, about 1/2 hour.   Using a butter knife or pastry brush, coat one side of matza with softened margarine. Generously sprinkle with sugar. Place four prepared matza in front of you, buttered side up, so that they are arranged to form a square. Turn your tart pan upside down over arranged matza squares. With a sharp knife cut around tart pan leaving a one inch border. You should have four matza wedges forming a circle. Now, turn tart pan right side up and place wedges with points at center of pan, coated side down, so that pan is covered forming a matza crust. Coat prepared matza inside pan with margarine, sprinkle with sugar.   Bake crust in preheated oven for about 10 minutes then cool, to allow crust to set well. While crust is baking, let's prepare the APPLE TART FILLING...

3	*Medium/Large Green Pippin Apples, Thinly Sliced*
1/2	*Cup Apricot Jam (Pureed If Available) (*Light)*
1/3	*Cup Walnuts, Roasted And Crushed*

Now, directly from the jar, take about two tablespoons of apricot jam, and using a butter knife spread the bottom of prepared COOLED tart shell with the jam. Sprinkle walnuts on top of the jam spread. Take your sliced apples and begin in the center by arranging them in a spiral formation and continue until you run out of apples. Now, place tart back into preheated oven for about 35 minutes or until apples and crust are golden.

While the tart is in the oven... In a small sized sauce pan heat the apricot jam and dissolve until it has liquefied. When the tart has browned, remove from the oven, and while still warm, evenly drizzle the jam over your apple tart. Completely cool, serve, and hear the OOH'S and AHH'S, and...ENJOY!

Matza Chocolate Berry Tart

Preheat Oven 400 Degrees - Preparation Time 30 Minutes - Yield 8

Our Chocolate Raspberry Creme Tart is definitely a "show piece" for the Passover Table. Fresh fruit, especially raspberries, incorporated with our chocolate cream and crisp matza crust, will definitely satisfy your sweet tooth and not weigh you down at the same time. You will need the following ingredients for our CHOCOLATE RASPBERRY CREME TART...

For Matza Cutting see Diagram 1	

4	*Prepared Matza*
3	*Tablespoons Margarine Or Butter, Softened (*Light)*
1/4	*Cup Orange Juice*
1/2	*Teaspoon Vanilla Extract*
1/4	*Cup Sugar*
1/4	*Cup Almonds, Toasted And Crushed*

Grease a 9" tart pan; sprinkle with some of the sugar and set aside. Combine orange juice and vanilla in a small spray bottle. Take prepared matza and spray both sides with orange juice/vanilla mixture. For better saturation, set matza aside for about 1/2 hour. Using a butter knife or pastry brush, coat both sides of matza with softened margarine and generously sprinkle both sides with sugar. Place four prepared matza in front of you so that they are arranged to form a square. Turn your tart pan upside down over arranged matza squares. With a sharp knife, cut around tart pan leaving a one inch border. You should have four matza wedges forming a circle. Now, turn tart pan right side up and place wedges with points at center of pan, so that pan is covered forming a matza crust. Place crushed, toasted almonds on bottom of matza crust, then sprinkle with remaining sugar. Bake crust in preheated oven for 20 minutes or until golden brown, cool. While crust is baking let's prepare CREME FILLING...

3.9	*Ounce Chocolate Instant Pudding Mix (One Small Box)*
3/4	*Cup Milk (*1% Lowfat)*
1/2	*Pint Real Whipping Cream (*Light)*
1	*Tablespoon Powdered Sugar*

Prepare instant pudding according to directions on package **EXCEPT USE ONLY 3/4 CUP MILK;** using a whisk to whip and set aside. Whip 1/2 pint real whipping cream, adding one tablespoon powdered sugar, whip until light and fluffy. Add pudding to whip cream and whip until pudding has been well whipped into cream, spread over baked matza crust. Now, for the TOPPING...

3	*Cups Fresh Raspberries*
1/3	*Cup Raspberry Jelly Plus 1 Teaspoon Water*

Arrange berries over tart, close together, beginning at outer edge of tart and circling toward the middle. In a small sauce pan, over low heat, combine jelly and water until smooth. Spoon or brush gently jelly mixture over raspberries and chill three to four hours...ENJOY!

Matza Fresh Fruit Tart

Preheat Oven 400 Degrees - Preparation Time 20 Minutes - Yield 8

Tarts, Tarts, Tarts! Yes, another delicious tart made with a crisp matza crust and filled with a lightly sweetened cream. What could be better? Not much, in our opinion. So, let's begin by preparing our FRESH FRUIT TART CRUST...

For Matza Cutting see Diagram 1	

4	*Prepared Matza*
3	*Tablespoons Margarine Or Buttered, Softened (*Light)*
1/4	*Cup Orange Juice*
1/2	*Teaspoon Vanilla Extract*
1/4	*Cup Sugar*
1/4	*Cup Almonds, Toasted And Crushed*

Grease a 9" tart pan, sprinkle with some of the sugar and set aside. Combine orange juice and vanilla in small spray bottle. Take prepared matza and spray both sides with orange juice/vanilla mixture. You can set matza aside to allow better saturation, about 1/2 hour. Using a butter knife or pastry brush, coat both sides of matza with softened margarine and generously sprinkle both sides with sugar. Place four prepared matza in front of you, so that they are arranged to form a square. Turn your tart pan upside down over arranged matza squares. With a sharp knife cut around tart pan leaving a one inch border. You should have four matza wedges forming a circle. Now, turn tart pan right side up and place wedges with points at center of pan, so that pan is covered forming a matza crust. Bake crust in preheated oven for about 20 minutes or until golden brown, cool. While crust is baking, prepare the CREAM FILLING...

3.4	*Ounce Of French Vanilla Instant Pudding Mix (Small Box)*
3/4	*Cup Milk (1% Lowfat)*
1/2	*Pint Real Whipping Cream (*Light)*
2	*Tablespoons Powdered Sugar*

Prepare the instant pudding according to directions on package **EXCEPT USE ONLY 3/4 CUP OF MILK**. Whip 1/2 pint of real whipping cream, adding 2 tablespoons of powdered sugar until light and fluffy. Add whipped cream mixture to the pudding mixture and whip together until light and fluffy and spread over baked matza crust. Now, we will get started on arranging the FRUIT TOPPING...

1	*Banana, Sliced AND 12 Strawberries, Sliced*
1	*Cup Seedless Grapes*
1/3	*Cup Strawberry Jelly Plus 1 Teaspoon Water*

Arrange banana, berries, and grapes over filling in circular pattern beginning with grapes circling the outer edge of the tart pan, then the berries, then the banana and finally, one whole berry in the center of tart for finishing garnish. In small sauce pan over low heat, combine jelly and water until smooth. Spoon over fruit and chill 3 to 4 hours...ENJOY!

Matza Maple Pecan Tart

Preheat Oven 450 Degrees - Preparation Time 30 Minutes - Yield 8

This tart has a great maple flavor with the rich nutty taste of pecans as the topping. It is also kosher for Passover because it is made without corn syrup. The maple flavor absolutely compliments our pecan-nutty matza crust. For your MAPLE PECAN TART you will need the following ingredients...

For Matza
Cutting see
Diagram 1

4	*Prepared Matza*
3	*Tablespoons Margarine Or Butter, Softened (*Light)*
1/4	*Cup Orange Juice*
1/2	*Teaspoon Vanilla Extract*
1/4	*Cup Sugar*
1/4	*Cup Pecans, Toasted And Finely Crushed*

Generously grease and sprinkle sugar on a 9" tart pan and set aside. Combine orange juice and vanilla in a small spray bottle. Spray both sides of prepared matza with orange juice/vanilla mixture. For better saturation, set matza aside for about 1/2 hour. Using a butter knife or pastry brush, generously spread margarine or butter on both sides of matza and generously sprinkle both sides with sugar. Place all four pieces of prepared matza in front of you so that they are arranged to form a square. Turn tart pan upside down over arranged matza squares. Using a sharp knife, cut around tart pan leaving a one inch border. You should now have four matza wedges with points in the center of the pan so that pan is well covered to form a matza crust. Sprinkle the bottom of the crust with both toasted pecans and sugar; set aside. Now, for the FILLING...

1	*Cup Maple Syrup (*Reduced Calorie)*
2	*Teaspoons Vanilla*
1/8	*Teaspoon Salt*
3	*Eggs (*2 Whole Eggs And 2 Egg Whites)*
1/2	*Cup Chopped Pecans*

In a medium sized mixing bowl, combine maple syrup, vanilla, salt, eggs and whisk until well mixed (mixture becomes light and a little frothy), then pour into Matza Crust. Sprinkle pecans over maple syrup mixture. Place tart on a baking sheet, (wrap baking sheet in aluminum foil to avoid a mess) and bake in preheated oven for ten minutes. Reduce heat to 325 degrees and bake for twenty more minutes or until filling is set. You need not serve with anything but coffee or tea because of its richness - Let cool completely...ENJOY!

Matza Peach Raspberry Tart

Preheat Oven 325 Degrees - Preparation Time 25 Minutes - Yield 8

Elegant deserting calls for a PEACH RASPBERRY TART that can be served with coffee either in the morning or mid-afternoon, and is definitely a great "pick me up" during anytime of the day...

	4	*Prepared Matza*
For Matza Cutting see Diagram 1	3	*Tablespoons Margarine, Softened (*Light)*
	1/4	*Cup EACH Orange Juice And Sugar*
	1/2	*Teaspoon Vanilla Extract*
	1/3	*Cup Toasted Almond Crumbs (Food Processed)*

Grease a 9" pie pan and sprinkle with sugar; set aside. Combine orange juice and vanilla in small spray bottle. Spray both sides of prepared matza with orange/juice vanilla mixture. You can set matza aside for better saturation, about 1/2 hour. Using a butter knife or pastry brush, coat both sides of matza with softened margarine and sprinkle both sides with sugar. Place all four prepared matzas in front of you, so that they are arranged to form a square. Turn the pie pan upside down over arranged matza squares. Using a sharp knife, cut around pie pan leaving a 1 inch border. You should now have four matza wedges forming a circle. Now, turn the pie pan right side up and place wedges with points in the center of pan so that pan is well covered to form a matza crust. Sprinkle the bottom of the crust with both toasted almonds and sugar and set aside. Now, let's gather the following ingredients for the FILLING...

3/4	*Cup Sugar, Plus 2 Tablespoons For Crumb Topping*
2	*Tablespoons EACH Matza Meal & Toasted Chopped Almonds*
1	*Tablespoons Butter, Softened (*Light)*
1/4	*Teaspoon Cinnamon*
3	*Cups Cream Cheese, Softened (*Light)*
1	*Teaspoon Vanilla*
3	*Eggs (*2 Whole Eggs And 2 Egg Whites)*
2 1/2	*Cups Canned Peaches, Sliced (16 Oz Can)*
1/2	*Cup Raspberries, Must Be Fresh*

In a small bowl, combine 2 tablespoons sugar, add the matza meal, butter, and cinnamon, chopped nuts and mix until crumbly; set aside. Combine cream cheese, 3/4 cup sugar and vanilla and with an electric mixer, on medium speed, mix until well blended. Add eggs and blend well. Pour cream cheese mixture into matza crust. Arrange peach slices over cheese filling, garnish with fresh raspberries, and lightly top with crumb topping. Bake filled tart in preheated oven for about one hour or until center is set. *COOL*. Refrigerate 3 hours or overnight...ENJOY!

Matza Strawberry Tarts

Preheat Oven 450 Oven - Preparation Time 30 Minutes - Yield 16

This is a must for serving... It is one of the most impressive recipes!!! Did we mention it's easy too? During our experimental stages, no one could believe that matza could be so manipulated. After this sweet tart shell is baked, you can basically fill with our cream cheese filling and top with fresh strawberries or peaches. Compliment with same type of jam. Once you've made tarts using matza, you will find yourself preparing tarts in this manner from now on -- *BECAUSE IT IS JUST THAT SIMPLE.* You will need the following ingredients for the TART SHELLS...

16	*Prepared Matza (Or 8 Prepared Matza For 32 Mini Tarts)*
1	*Cup Orange Juice*
1	*Tablespoon Vanilla Extract*
3/4	*Cup Sugar*
8	*Tablespoons Margarine, Softened (*Light)*

Combine orange juice and vanilla in small spray bottle. Take prepared matza and spray both sides with orange juice/vanilla mixture. You can set matza aside to allow better saturation, about 1/2 hour. Cut prepared, flavored matza to 5" inch rounds (typical cereal bowl size). Coat small tart pans with margarine and sprinkle with sugar. Brush both sides of matza rounds generously with margarine, and generously sprinkle both sides with sugar, and finally gently press matza round into place in tart pan. Place tart pans onto large cookie sheets for baking in preheated oven for about 12 to 15 minutes or until lightly browned and crisp. Set aside, and let cool. *NOTE: Tart shells will remain crisp if browned thoroughly -- if tart shells are removed from oven to soon, they will be soft and remain soft.* Now for the FILLING...

For Matza Cutting see Page 32		
For mini tarts	*4*	*Cups Cream Cheese, Softened (*Light)*
	1 1/2	*Cups Butter, Or Margarine (*Light)*
	3	*Cups Powdered Sugar*
	4	*Teaspoons Vanilla*
	6	*Baskets Firm Strawberries (About 8-10 Cups)*
	1	*Cup Strawberry Jam (*Low Cal)*

In medium sized mixing bowl, combine together cream cheese, butter, sugar and vanilla and thoroughly whip until light and fluffy. Generously fill cooled tarts with cream cheese filling. Arrange strawberries on top of each tart with pointed side up. Melt strawberry jam, cool to a stirrable consistency and drizzle about one tablespoon over strawberry tops. The purpose for letting the jam cool after it has melted, is to avoid cream cheese filling from curdling and strawberries from getting soft. Now, be prepared to receive the greatest of compliments for a gourmet type recipe and gloat as the impressive hostess. ANOTHER *easy alternative is to substitute the tart pans for muffin tins and top the tarts with only one strawberry as a topping or fresh fruit of the season. Each matza should yield 9-2" bite size tarts. Once matza is seasoned and cut, you will gently tuck into muffin tins. You'll find this method makes an ample individual serving - from us to you...ENJOY!*

Matza Brownie Walnut Pie

Preheat Oven 325 Degrees - Preparation Time 25 Minutes - Yield 8

For brownie lovers, this pie is it! This exclusive recipe is a chocolates lover's dream dessert that can be served after dinner with coffee or tea, as well as in the afternoon with a glass of milk. We believe that with the combination of chocolate and cream cheese, topped off with our crunchy chocolate chip/walnut topping and lined by a beautifully thin matza crust. Well, every bite of this BROWNIE WALNUT PIE will just absolutely melt in your mouth!

For Matza Cutting see Diagram 1	

4   ***Prepared Matza***

3   ***Tablespoons Margarine, Softened (*Light)***

1/4   ***Cup <u>EACH</u> Orange Juice And Sugar***

1/2   ***Teaspoon Vanilla Extract***

1/3   ***Cup Toasted Walnuts (Food Processed)***

Lightly grease 9" pie pan with margarine, lightly sprinkle with sugar, set aside. Combine orange juice and vanilla in small spray bottle. Spray both sides of prepared matza with orange/juice vanilla mixture. You can set matza aside for better saturation, about 1/2 hour. Using a butter knife or pastry brush, coat both sides of matza with softened margarine and sprinkle both sides with sugar. Place all four prepared matzas in front of you, so that they are arranged to form a square. Turn the pie pan upside down over arranged matza squares. Using a sharp knife, cut around pie pan leaving a 1 inch border. You should now have four matza wedges forming a circle. Now, turn the pie pan right side up and place wedges with points in the center of pan so that pan is well covered to form a matza crust. Sprinkle the bottom of the crust with both toasted walnuts and sugar and set aside. Now, let's gather the following ingredients for the FILLING...

3   ***Cups Cream Cheese, Softened (24 Oz.) (*Light)***

1/3   ***Cup Un-Sweetened Cocoa Powder***

1   ***Cup Sugar***

1   ***Teaspoon Vanilla***

3   ***Eggs (*2 Whole Eggs And 2 Egg Whites)***

1   ***Cup Chocolate Chips (1/4 Cup Reserved For Garnish)***

3/4   ***Cup Walnuts, Chopped***

In medium sized mixing bowl combine cream cheese, cocoa powder, sugar, and vanilla and with an electric mixer, on medium speed, mix until well blended. Add eggs and blend well. Pour chocolate cream cheese mixture into matza crust. Sprinkle 3/4 cup of the chocolate chips and toasted walnuts over pie and bake in preheated oven for about one hour or until center is set.. *COOL*. Garnish top of pie by drizzling about 1/4 cup melted chocolate chips. Refrigerate 3 hours or overnight...ENJOY!

Matza Lemon Meringue Pie

Stove Top/Preheat Oven 400 Degrees - Prep Time 30 Minutes - Yield 8

You will find that our matza pie crust is adaptable for any pie. We chose lemon meringue pie because of the ease involved in preparation and its showy presentation. Lets gather these ingredients for LEMON MERINGUE PIE...

4	*Prepared Matza*
1/4	*Cup Orange Juice*
1/2	*Teaspoon Vanilla Extract*
3	*Tablespoons Margarine, Softened (*Light)*
1/4	*Cup __EACH__ Sugar And Almonds, Toasted & Finely Crushed*

For Matza Cutting see Diagram 1

Grease a 9" pie pan and sprinkle with sugar; set aside. Combine orange juice and vanilla in small spray bottle. Spray both sides of prepared matza with orange/juice vanilla mixture. You can set matza aside for better saturation, about 1/2 hour. Using a butter knife or pastry brush, coat both sides of matza with softened margarine and sprinkle both sides with sugar. Place all four prepared matzas in front of you, so that they are arranged to form a square. Turn the pie pan upside down over arranged matza squares. Using a sharp knife, cut around pie pan leaving a 1 inch border. You should now have four matza wedges forming a circle. Now, turn the pie pan right side up and place wedges with points in the center of pan so that pan is well covered to form a matza crust. Sprinkle the bottom of the crust with both toasted almonds and sugar. Bake the crust in a preheated oven for about 15 minutes or until golden brown. FILLING...

1 1/3	*Cup Sugar (Set 1/3 Cup Aside For Meringue Topping)*
1/3	*Cup Plus 1 Tablespoon Potato Starch*
1 1/2	*Cups Water*
3	*Egg Yolks, Beaten (Save Egg Whites For Meringue Topping)*
3	*Tblsp Margarine (Use Butter For Richer Pie) (*Light)*
2	*Teaspoons Lemon Peel*
1/2	*Cup Freshly Squeezed Lemon Juice*
1	*Teaspoon Vanilla (Used For Meringue Topping)*

Not over heat, in medium sized sauce pan combine sugar and potato starch and **mix well.** Gradually add water, stir until sugar has dissolved. Now, cook this mixture over medium heat until thickened; constantly stirring. When mixture boils, turn heat off, add beaten eggs and continue to stir until well mixed.   Turn heat back on, continue to stir until mixture boils, remove from heat. Stir in the margarine, lemon peel, lemon juice, and pour hot mixture into baked matza crust. In bowl beat 3 egg whites and vanilla, adding 1 tablespoon sugar at a time and beat until stiff and glossy Spoon meringue over hot filling, bake for 10 minutes or until top is light brown, cool...ENJOY!

Matza Pear/Apple Crumb Pie

Preheat Oven 425 Degrees - Preparation Time 25 Minutes - Yield 8

This is a "Not-to-sweet recipe" and takes on the natural sweet flavor from the apples and pears. You will need the following ingredients for APPLE CRUMB PIE...

For Matza Cutting see Diagram 1	

4	*Prepared Matza*
3	*Tablespoons Margarine, Softened (*Light)*
1/4	*Cup Orange Juice*
1/2	*Teaspoon Vanilla Extract*
1/4	*Cup Sugar*
1/4	*Cup Almonds, Toasted And Crushed*

Grease a 10" pie pan and sprinkle with some of the sugar; set aside. Combine orange juice and vanilla in small spray bottle. Spray both sides of prepared matza with orange/juice vanilla mixture. You can set matza aside for better saturation, about 1/2 hour. Using a butter knife or pastry brush, coat both sides of matza with softened margarine and sprinkle both sides with sugar. Place all four prepared matzas in front of you, so that they are arranged to form a square. Turn the pie pan upside down over arranged matza squares. Using a sharp knife, cut around pie pan leaving a 1 inch border. You should now have four matza wedges forming a circle. Now, turn the pie pan right side up and place wedges with points in the center of pan so that pan is well covered to form a matza crust. Sprinkle the bottom of the crust with both toasted almonds and remaining sugar and set aside. Now, let's gather the following ingredients for the FILLING...

2	*Large Pippin Or Granny Smith Apples (About 2 Pounds)*
2	*Large Pears (About 2 Pounds)*
1	*Tablespoon Lemon Juice*

Cut the apples and pears into thin slices. Sprinkle lemon juice over fruit (to not brown). Place alternate layers of pears and apples into crust. Cover with the following ingredients for the TOPPING...

8	*Tablespoons Margarine Or Butter (*Light)*
1	*Teaspoon Vanilla*
1	*Cup Matza Meal*
1/2	*Cup Sugar*
1//4	*Teaspoon Of Cinnamon*
3/4	*Cup Almonds, Toasted And Crushed*
1/3	*Cup Honey*

Mix all of the ingredients well and crumble over the Pear/Apple pie. Bake in preheated oven for 30 minutes or until nicely browned. This pie tastes scrumptious when served warm out of the oven. This is definitely a pie that can be served a-la-mode (vanilla ice cream)...ENJOY!

Matza Walnut Wheels

Preheat Oven 400 Degrees - Preparation Time 20 Minutes - Yield 24

For a nice chewy bite, with that slight walnutty taste, we would suggest these WHEELS and even try serving on a platter as a compliment with our many other cookies...

6	*Prepared Matza*
4	*Tablespoons Margarine Or Butter, Softened (*Light)*
1/2	*Cup Sugar*
1/2	*Cub Orange Juice*
1/2	*Teaspoon Vanilla Extract*

Generously margarine two large cookie sheets and generously sprinkle some of the sugar onto cookie sheets. Combine orange juice and vanilla in a small spray bottle and spray both sides of matza with orange juice/ vanilla mixture. For better saturation, set matza aside for 1/2 hour. Using a pastry brush or butter knife, brush both sides of matza generously with margarine and sprinkle generously both sides of matza with sugar. Now, take one piece of prepared matza and with a round cookie cutter, approximately three inches in diameter, cut four circles per matza and place circles onto prepared cookie sheets. Repeat this process for all remaining matza. Bake for 15 minutes or until golden brown. ***DO NOT OVER BAKE, or MATZA ROUNDS WILL TASTE BITTER.*** Remove from oven and let cool completely before removing from cookie sheets. When completely cooled, place matza rounds on buttered rack. Now, we will prepare the WALNUT WHEEL TOPPING...

3/4 -1	*Cup Whole Toasted Walnuts (Halves)*
2	*Cup Brown Sugar, Packed*
1	*Tablespoons Water*
3/4 -1	*Cup Raisins, For Topping*
1/2	*Dark Chocolate Chips, Melted (Used To Lightly Drizzling) (*Reduced Fat)*

Place three walnuts and raisins in center of matza round that is cooling on buttered rack. Heat brown sugar and water in a small sauce pan over low heat until melted. Bring this mixture to a boil and boil for about one to two minutes, stirring constantly. Remove from heat and drizzle over cookies topped with walnuts and raisins. Cover entire cookie with this mixture to secure walnuts to the cookie; let set for about 1/2 hour. Finally, lightly drizzle with melted chocolate...ENJOY!

Diagrams 1 - 3

Diagram #1

Diagram #2

Diagram #3

Diagrams 4 - 6

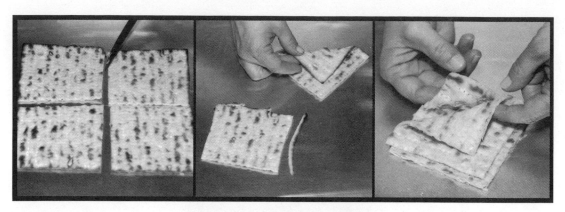

Diagram #4

Diagram #5

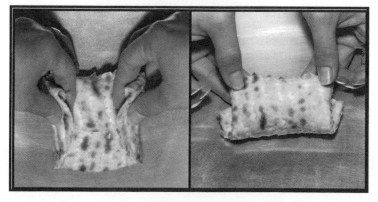

Diagram #6

Diagrams 7 - 8

Diagram #7

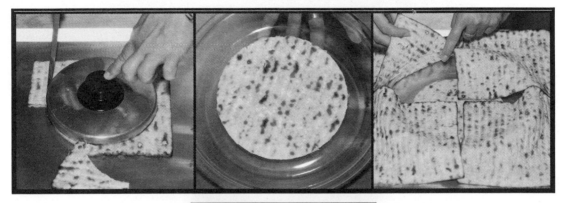

Diagram #8

Diagrams 9 - 11

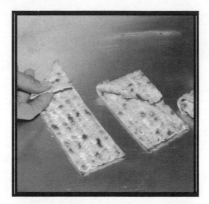

Diagram #9

Diagram #10

Diagram #11

Diagrams 12 - 14

Diagram #12

Diagram #13

Diagram #14

Diagrams 15 - 16

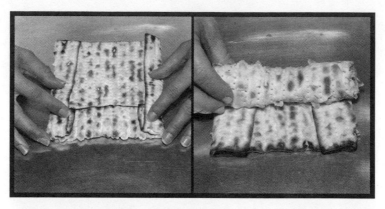

Diagram #15

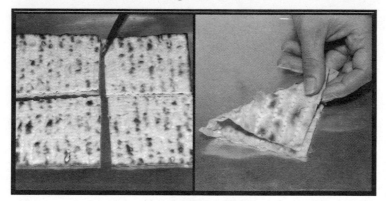

Diagram #16

Index

Almond cookies, 104

Almond squares, 105

Apple/cinnamon broilers, 107

Apple strudel, 106

Apple tart, 137

Asparagus crispers, 48

Asparagus rolls, 73

Asparagus Swiss quiche, 56

Baklava, 108

Banana blintzes, 59

Banana nut broilers, 109

Beef 'n' potato turnovers, 92

Beef pot pies, 93

Borekas, 76

Breakfast spirals, 75

Brei, 66

Brei savory style, 67

Broccoli cheese casserole, 52

Broccoli quiche, 57

Brownie walnut pie, 143

Sugar cookies, 110

Cannelloni, 53

Cannolies, 112

Cheese blintzes, 61

Cheese cake, 135

Cheese casserole, 45

Cheese lasagna, 42

Cheese star appetizers, 77

Cherry jubilee cookies, 117

Chicken bastilla, 99

Chicken bastilla flags, 98

Chicken pot pies, 100

Chili pepper chicken, 97

Chili pepper rellenos, 54

Chocolate berry tart, 138

Chocolate cherry bars, 113

Chocolate chip cookies, 114

Chocolate clusters, 115

Chocolate glazed cookies, 116

Cinnamon toast popovers, 74

Cream cheese 'n' onion bakes, 78

Cream cheese surprises, 79

Crystallized nuts, 111

Date mousse puffs, 118

Egg folds, 49

Eggplant lasagna, 43

Florentines, 119

Fondue strips, 120

Fruit kugel, 62

Fruit pancakes, 64

Fruit tart, 139

Garlic parmesan, 80

Garlic teasers, 81

Gefilte fish enchiladas, 44

Haroseth cookie rolls, 121

Honey chewies, 122

Honey nut strudel, 123

*I*ce Cream Sandwiches, 133

*J*alapeno pockets, 82

Jammer Cookies, 124

*L*asagna Spinach Rolls, 51

Lemon meringue pie, 144

*M*aple `n` nut crunch, 125

Maple pecan tart, 140

Meat cigars, 94

Meat knishes, 96

Mini franks, 95

Mozzarella melts, 83

*N*apoleon, 126

Newtons, 127

*P*each raspberry tart, 141

Pear/apple crumb pie, 145

Pears al-dente, 60

Pecan brown sugar crunchies, 128

Pineapple strudel, 129

Pizza pizza squares, 84

Pizzzz-a pockets, 85

Potato knishes, 46

*S*almon carousels, 68

Salmon pockets, 69

Salsa cream cheese mousse, 86

Savory pancakes, 65

Sesame teasers, 130

Spinach quiche, 58

Spring rolls, 87

Strawberry tarts, 142

Stuffers, Italian style, 50

Sweet kugel, 63

T aco shells, 88

Taiglach, 131

Tex-mex chicken, 101

Tortilla chips, 89

Tuna bakes, 71

Tuna casserole, 70

Tuna tostadas, 72

Turkey rolls, 102

V anilla crisps, 132

Vegetable cheese quesadilla, 55

Veggie calzones, 47

W alnut bon bons, 134

Walnut Wheels, 146

Cook's Notes

Cook's Notes